T0097542

⇒ Homemade ⇐

COOKBOOKS BY BEATRICE OJAKANGAS
Published by the University of Minnesota Press

The Great Holiday Baking Book
Great Old-Fashioned American Desserts
Great Old-Fashioned American Recipes
The Great Scandinavian Baking Book
Great Whole Grain Breads
Pot Pies
Quick Breads
Scandinavian Cooking
Scandinavian Feasts

Homemade

FINNISH RYE, FEED SACK FASHION, AND OTHER
SIMPLE INGREDIENTS FROM MY LIFE IN FOOD

BEATRICE OJAKANGAS

University of Minnesota Press

Minneapolis • London

Published by the University of Minnesota Press
111 Third Avenue South, Suite 290
Minneapolis, MN 55401-2520
http://www.upress.umn.edu

Printed in the United States of America on acid-free paper

The University of Minnesota is an equal-opportunity educator and employer.

30 29 28 27 26 25 24 23 22   10 9 8 7 6 5 4 3 2

Library of Congress Cataloging-in-Publication Data
Ojakangas, Beatrice, author.
Homemade : Finnish rye, feed sack fashion, and other simple ingredients from my life in food /
Beatrice Ojakangas.
Minneapolis : University of Minnesota Press, [2016]
Identifiers: LCCN 2016027973 | ISBN 978-0-8166-9579-9 (hc)
Subjects: LCSH: Cooking, Finnish. | Cooking—Minnesota. | Ojakangas, Beatrice. | LCGFT: Cookbooks.
Classification: LCC TX723.5.F5 O42 2016 | DDC 641.59776—dc23
LC record available at https://lccn.loc.gov/2016027973

Contents

Acknowledgments   ix

Prologue: Any Questions?   xi

◆ PART I

My Paternal Grandparents: A Story of Commitment and Perseverance   3
  Finnish Cardamom Coffee Bread (Pulla)   6
  Korppu   7

My Maternal Grandparents: A Story of Famine, Fire, and Fear   8
  Grandmother's Sugar Cookies   12

First Names First   15
  Finnish-Style Mojakka   17

Growing Up on a Farm in Northern Minnesota   18

Salt Cake   22
  Mummy's Simple White Cake   23

There Were Ten of Us   25

Being Finnish   31
  Thin Finnish Pancakes (Lattyja)   34

Sunday Services at Uncle Frank's   35

Summers on the Farm   37
  Wild Berry Jam   38

Swimming   39

Cows in Wintertime   41
  Finnish Baked Cheese (Leipäjuusto)   45

Venison   46
  The Best Venison Liver and Onions   47

Visits from Aunts and Uncles   48
    Orange Date-Nut Cake   53

My Twelfth Birthday   54

No Recipe Needed   56
    Mummy's "Juicy" Cinnamon Rolls   57

Feed Sack Fashion   58

Hired Men   61
    Mrs. Long's Graham Rieska   63

Christmas Trees   64
    Pulla People   66

Some Stories Are Hard to Tell   68

Vesala   70

Floodwood, My Hometown   72
    Sam's Socklat Cake   74

Lincoln School in Floodwood   76

Anne Brown's Beauty Parlor   80

Town Kids versus Country Kids   82
    Country Carrot Meatloaf   83

Seeds for a Bible   84

Heaven and How to Get There   86

Confirmation in the Finnish Lutheran Church   88

Till the Cows Come Home   90

The End-of-Summer Prize   92
    Lemon or Orange Chiffon Cake   96

Back to the State Fair   97
    Cheese Soufflé   99
    Finnish Rye Bread   101

◆ **PART II**

Becoming a Home Economist   105

A Turn in the Road   108

My First Taste of Gourmet Food   111
    Hot Cheese Puffs   *112*
    Burnt Sugar Ice Cream   *113*

My "Toast in the Morning Man"   115
    Almond Cardamom Scones   *118*

The Pillsbury Bake-Off   119
    Cheesy Picnic Bread (Chunk o' Cheese Bread)   *123*

A Year in Finland   124
    Lanttulaatikko (Rutabaga Casserole)   *125*
    Swedish Prince's (Princess) Cake   *126*

Stories from Finland   129
    May Day Tippaleipä   *132*
    Sima   *133*

Sunset Magazine   134

A Marriage Encounter with Moussaka   136
    Moussaka   *136*

A Food Writer and a Mom   139
    Jumbo Sugar Jumbles   *140*

Welcome Back to Duluth   141

Somebody's House   145
    Rabbitburger   *148*
    Stroganoff Burger   *149*
    Swiss Fondue   *149*

Jeno and the Big Idea   150

Two Years at Vocational School   152
    Karjalan Paisti (Karelian Three-Meat Stew)   *153*

Cooking School in the South of France with Simca   155
    Tarte de Nancy   *156*
    Pâté Sucrée   *157*

Nice Is Nice   158
    A Totally Untraditional Bouillabaisse   160

The Seven-Course Morel Festival Meal   162
    Cream of Morel Soup   163

In the Kitchen with Julia Child   165
    Quick Method Danish Pastry   167
    Danish Pastry Braid   168

On TV with Martha Stewart   169
    Katja's Birthday Sponge Cake   172

Peachie, the Butter Spokesperson   174

Cookie Questions   176
    Chocolate Chip Cookies   177

The Great River Road   178
    Nauvoo Wheat-Nut Coffeecake   179
    Shrimp à la Creole   180

The Butter Churn and My Beloved Mom   181

Twenty-Nine Cookbooks and Counting—All of Them "Pot Boilers"   183

Cooking in a Church Kitchen (Bring Sharp Knives!)   193
    Three-Grain Wild Rice Sunflower Seed Bread   195

Summing It Up   196

Acknowledgments

From the poetry of Alfred, Lord Tennyson, I recognize a basic truth that "I am a part of all I have met." From my family to my friends and to the teachers, both formal and in passing, I owe a debt of thanks and acknowledgment. My life is more than what I have inherited through blood and body. I have had the incredible support of extended family and friends, who somehow magically appear just when I need encouragement the most.

This is for you, my family. To my late mother, Esther Honkala Luoma, who taught me to cook on the woodstove, and my late father, Ted, who put ingenuity into my gene pool. To my husband, Dick; kids, Cathy, Greg, Susanna; and my grandkids, who are "grand" indeed: Niko, Tomas, Isabella, Kieran, Celka, Lian, Frans, and Kaisa. My hope is that these stories will shed a bit of light on each of you. Also, for my nine brothers and sisters and countless cousins, there may be something here that explains some mysterious family trait.

To the folks at the University of Minnesota Press, who have been so amazingly supportive—Erik Anderson, Kristian Tvedten, and others: I couldn't have done it without you!

Any Questions?

I have just completed a cooking demonstration, maybe on holiday baking or on the many ways to use rhubarb or some other item of current interest. I've mixed, chopped, cleaned, sautéed, and measured, explaining the function of each ingredient and the techniques I find work best. I've led others through the process, we share ideas, and I end the presentation with a call for questions. While I'm expecting to answer inquiries about the product at hand and what we have just been discussing, instead the first question is almost always "How did you get into writing cookbooks?" Then, the familiar questions follow: "What was Julia like?" or "What is Martha really like?"

I like to start at the beginning. Ever since I was a young girl, growing up on a farm in northern Minnesota, I wanted to write. Books fascinated me, how they could transport the reader to another land by words alone. I wanted to write about all kinds of things. I wrote stories but knew little about how the outside world worked. Food eventually became an easy topic for me; I learned to cook and bake before I could read—and on a woodstove! A few years later (and concocting a way to get a few days of vacation in the summer) I officially began my foods career through the local 4-H, where I won trips to the State Fair through cooking demonstrations. It launched a whole new world for me.

To be honest, to think about writing my own memoir seems self-serving. I didn't ever believe I would be noticed or that what I had to say would be held credible by anyone. I've always felt "hidden behind the bushes" because of where I live. Nobody seems to hear about northern Minnesota unless it is weather related. The icebox of the nation. The land of lakes, wolves, bears, swamps, and mosquitoes. Who could be interested in that?

And yet I have always had this overwhelming desire to talk—to write—to tell people about my life. Though it really wasn't ever about *me*: it is about what surrounds me. The beauty of this northern place, the love of friends and family, the funny and incredible things that have happened to me in the little bubble in which I dwell. And always, through everything, food. Growing up on the farm, I would talk to the animals, to the trees, even to a blade of grass. I found a piece of paper so beautiful I would become emotional and attribute to it a flavor, a color—and it became a thing of beauty. The best gift I could receive was a tablet with lines for writing.

The stories that follow are snippets of life growing up on a simple farm in northern Minnesota. I begin with stories about my grandparents, all four of whom immigrated from Finland and whose heritage has left a lasting impression on who I am and how I approach life and food. Throughout these stories, I usually refer to my mother as "Mummy" and my father as "Isä" (Finnish for father). There are stories of growing up on the farm, and then seeing a larger world unfold in front of my eyes through my love of food, from State Fair blue ribbons and national championship recipes to the Pillsbury Bake-Off, working for the wonderful California-based magazine *Sunset* in its food department, traveling to Finland to research cuisine and then returning to Duluth, where I helped invent the Jeno's Pizza Roll. And there are stories of later adventures in cooking, of meeting Julia Child and Martha Stewart. To this day it all still grows from the simple approaches to food that became such an important part of who I was growing up on the farm.

I'm 100 percent Finnish. That means all of my ancestors came from Finland. I'm also 100 percent Minnesotan, if I can be 100 percent of two different things. In Minnesota, we're trained to be what's called "Minnesota nice," and I'm not quite sure where that comes from. It could be that we're plunked in the middle of "New Scandinavia," but of course Finns aren't really Scandinavians. We're "Nordic," and that's what Scandinavians are, too. We're taught to "get along" with non-Lutherans. Nobody is wrong, they're just different. My mother made it very clear when I was growing up that regardless of skin color or personal differences, we are all equally loved. I am a child of God, as is everybody else. I was reminded later in life that when the Protestant Reformation was brought to Finland by Mikael Agricola, it was difficult to convince Finns that God could understand Finnish.

My husband is also 100 percent Finnish. That means our three kids are 100 percent Finnish. But our grandchildren are either 50 percent Finnish or 0 percent Finnish. Three of our eight grandchildren were adopted from Colombia. They are easy to spot in a crowd of Minnesotans because of their gorgeous, thick, dark hair and flashing dark eyes. The other five grandchildren are blond, fair-skinned, tall, and lanky, with soft brown or blue-green eyes.

"Who am I?" I have pondered this as I walk through our beautiful woods that are permeated with the aroma of poplar and evergreens. That's the underlying question as I begin writing. The thought comes to me time after time, something I learned early: "I am a part of all I have met." Just recently I took a course in which we were challenged to remember events both recent and past. The professor teaching the course commented that everything that has ever happened during a lifetime is recorded in the brain. What a remarkable fact! The happenings stored within my skull, then, add up to who I am.

Memories, both happy and sad, float to the top and create something beautiful, challenging, and heartbreaking. These memories strike a balance in my mind between thankfulness and opportunity.

Compassion for those less fortunate gives me pause. Stories about the difficulty my grandparents faced coming to this country and the struggles they experienced make my life seem like a total gift. Even within my own family I wonder why I have been so lucky, with a healthy body, sharp hearing, and clear sight while others endure deafness, blurred vision, muscular dystrophy, and other ailments. For these blessings I am thankful.

What follows are snippets from my life, memories of food and the farm and family, stories of the challenges I have faced and places I have traveled. And always: stories about food. These many ingredients create the recipe that makes me who I am.

= Part I =

Part I

My Paternal Grandparents

A Story of Commitment and Perseverance

I often wonder who I would be if my father's mother had married the man she loved. Susanna Kaisa Herneshuhta (or Sanna, as everyone called her) was born in 1872 in Lapua, Finland. I knew her only as a very old woman. She was eighty-one years old when she died. The last time I saw her, in 1957, I had walked the twenty blocks from my university dorm room at the University of Minnesota Duluth to the county hospital. Her thin white hair was pulled back, and her big, watery blue eyes seemed to see right through me. There was a calm about her that I couldn't explain.

Grandma, whom we called "Mummu," spent her last days in Miller Hospital in Duluth. She had been hospitalized because she had developed infections. I had just enough money to buy her a single rose. She loved roses. I wonder if her love for roses was because her birthday was at the end of June, just when the wild roses were in bloom. Her son Isä (my father, also known as Ted) loved roses, too, and planted many varieties in a long, narrow flower bed in the yard of our farmhouse in Floodwood, the small town fifty miles west of Duluth where I grew up.

Mummu had years earlier stepped into a posthole, fallen, and broken her hip. She was bedridden from that point on, as there was no such thing then as the hip replacement surgery so common today. I quietly slipped into the stark, antiseptic room and approached her in her narrow hospital bed. She was preaching sermons in Finnish. I could understand her, but nobody else could. I told her that nobody knew what she was talking about. Her answer was simply (in Finnish), "When God's word is preached in good, clear Finnish, anybody can understand it."

When I was growing up in Floodwood, Mummu would visit us, as she did all of her children. For her to "visit" meant that she would be staying with us for at least three months at a time. She didn't have a home of her own for the last twenty years of her life—except for the homes of her children. Her eldest son, Frank, according to tradition took over the farm after Grandpa died in 1933, the year before I was born. When she was with us, she was assigned to the "side bedroom" just off the living room. That was because she couldn't climb stairs anymore, and it was easy for her to go out and get fresh air on the porch.

When Mummu came to visit, she brought her belongings in a brown paper bag. I remember that she often wore more than one dress at a time, one on top of the other. Her breath was always sour and she smelled mildly of ammonia—like so many old people.

My father, Isä, bore a striking resemblance to her, with his slightly off-kilter-shaped head, high hairline, long, narrow nose, and oversized, almost bulging eyes. When my father died in 1997, in his late eighties, I thought he looked just like his mother.

Sanna had been in love with a young Lutheran pastor named Gustaf, who left for America when she was eighteen years old. Gustaf had promised to send her a ticket for passage to America as soon as he could save enough money.

Not far from Sanna's village, Lapua, is Ylistaro, also known as "the village with the beautiful church." The huge church was built, much to the amazement of the villagers, by the order of the czar in St. Petersburg, who controlled the building of all churches in the country. (Finland had been part of the Russian Empire since 1809.) The story went that the czar got his orders mixed up, and some large town somewhere got a tiny church that should have been built in Ylistaro. In truth, the church was indeed intended for Ylistaro because it is situated in the center of the parish. Sanna visited that impressive church as a young girl, and it was in this village that she met another young man named Konstant Luoma. It was hard times in Finland, about 1890, and men and women in their early teens and twenties, including Konstant, were leaving in great numbers to come to America, where the streets, they had heard, were paved with gold. Immigrants in the New World had to be resourceful. Practical skills and a strong back turned out to be the best assets a Finn could have.

Sanna had waited for her ticket from her beloved Gustaf for two years. Just as she was about to lose hope of ever getting to America, she received a letter from Konstant with a ticket and a proposal. She waited a few months more and finally wrote him, saying that she would accept his ticket and consenting to marry him. It took a few months to get everything together. She packed her belongings into a small trunk, and just days before embarking on her journey, she received a letter and a ticket from Gustaf. Heartbroken, Sanna continued with her plan to marry Konstant because she had made a promise. She returned Gustaf's ticket and used the ticket from Konstant to come to America in the late 1890s. She married Konstant and lived on the homesteaded farm he had carved out of the forest in Cedar Valley, Minnesota, about fifty miles northwest of Duluth. She bore him eleven children, including my father, Theodore, whom we called Isä. There was no way to connect with Gustaf, as Sanna had no idea where he was living.

Konstant died in 1933. Sanna wrote to her only living daughter, my aunt

Esther, saying that Gustaf had finally found her and had come to visit. He had spent his life as pastor of a small Lutheran church in Embarrass, Minnesota, less than a hundred miles from where Sanna and Konstant lived, yet a considerable distance given the lack of roads. Gustaf had married and had five children. His wife died earlier that same year.

Sanna and Gustaf sat at the trestle table in the farmhouse kitchen. Over a pot of coffee and freshly baked sweet coffee bread, the two discussed their lives for hours.

Sanna told Gustaf that Konstant had been a good provider. He was a hardworking, rough, strong, hard-drinking, but resourceful man who was able to make a living with his own two hands and a team of horses. Along with farming and logging, he cleared the forest to pave the way for roads and highways through that part of northern Minnesota.

It had not been an easy life for Sanna. According to Finnish tradition, the women took care of the animals and gardens and anything to do with the production and preparation of food. The men did the fertilizing and plowing of the fields. It was a woman's job to feed and milk the cows, clean the barn, and tend the vegetable gardens. Women helped with the haymaking. It made no difference that a woman might be pregnant. Babies were born at home with the help of the township's midwife.

Gustaf, on the other hand, lived in a home provided by his small Lutheran parish. Most of his salary was in the form of food and housing. There wasn't much cash for discretionary spending. He and his family couldn't travel, and they were under constant scrutiny from the village. Physically, life for Sanna would have been easier had she married Gustaf, who was a tender, loving pastor and much loved by the people in his congregation.

Sanna had longed for a life of spirituality, the life of a pastor's wife—especially when Konstant had come home in his swashbuckling way smelling of drink. She had spent her life in prayer for patience.

After their long talk comparing their lives, Sanna wrote to her daughter Esther to say that she and Gustaf had decided not to marry. It was too late. "I will die with the love of Gustaf in my heart," she wrote.

My aunt Esther cried.

I still wonder who I would be if Sanna had married Gustaf. I'll never know, nor would I want to know. My grandfather—who taught his boys to roll their own cigarettes at the age of eight—put resourcefulness, energy, creativity, and a sense of independence into my gene pool. Sanna mellowed all that out with her quiet and steady faith in God. Though Grandpa might not have spent much time in prayer, he lived in the service of his family, neighbors, and community—never denying the presence of God, but never one to sermonize, either. It really doesn't matter.

Finnish Cardamom Coffee Bread (Pulla)

We call this cardamom-perfumed bread "pulla," although Finns today might call it "biscuit," which irritated my Finnish aunt Ida. Other Finns called this bread "nisu" and even today there is some controversy among Finnish descendants. *Nisu*, it turns out, is the old Swedish name for wheat. When Finnish was "Finni-sized" in the early 1900s, the word *nisu* was changed to *vehnä*, the Finnish word for wheat. I have found this bread in Finland today being called "vehnäleipä" or wheat bread. I like to call it "pulla," even though the root name comes from the Swedish *bollar*. Whatever the name, the tender-crumbed, mildly sweet, cardamom-flavored bread is a standard in our house. This is my favorite recipe:

2 packages or 2 tablespoons active dry yeast
½ cup warm water, 105°F to 110°F
1 cup sugar
2 cups milk, scalded and cooled to lukewarm
1 teaspoon salt
1½ teaspoons freshly crushed cardamom seeds*
5 large eggs, 1 egg reserved for glaze
8 to 9 cups all-purpose flour
½ cup (1 stick) butter, softened
3 to 4 tablespoons pearl sugar** or sliced almonds for tops of loaves

In a large bowl, dissolve the yeast in the warm water and add about 1 teaspoon of the sugar. Set aside until the yeast begins to foam, about 5 minutes. Add the milk, salt, cardamom, 4 eggs, and 2–3 cups of the flour. Beat until very smooth and no lumps remain in the mixture. Slowly stir in 2 cups more flour until it is well blended into the batter. Stir in the softened butter. Set aside for about 15 minutes until the dough begins to rise a little. Stir in remaining flour to make a dough that is too stiff to stir easily. Turn out onto a floured board. Knead gently for 10 minutes until very smooth. Or, if you prefer (and this is what I do these days), turn the dough into the bowl of a standing mixer and knead using the dough hook, for 10 minutes until very smooth and satiny. TIP: Be stingy with the flour to make the most delicious, moist pulla. The final dough should still be "tacky" to the touch and a bit soft. Cover, and let rise until dough has doubled, about 1 hour.

Turn dough out onto a very lightly greased counter or worktable. Divide into three parts, and then divide each part into three. I sometimes dust the counter-top with a very light coating of flour to keep dough from sticking, although oiling the counter lightly helps, too. Shape each part of the dough into strands about 20 inches long (nine strands in all). Braid three strands at a time into a plait. Place on a greased cookie sheet, preferably one without sides. You will make three braids. Cover lightly with a towel and let rise for about 45 minutes to 1 hour.

Preheat the oven to 325°F. Beat the remaining egg and brush each loaf carefully, coating the tops and sides. Sprinkle with pearl sugar and/or sliced almonds. Bake for 20 to 25 minutes until light golden-brown. Do not overbake. Cool on racks and slice to serve.

* Cardamom: This is the third-most expensive spice, just behind saffron and vanilla. I suppose my grandmother brought the spice with her from Finland and kept it carefully guarded because of its value. The spice was popularly used for flavoring specialty baking, especially coffee bread in Finland. Her reunion with Gustaf was a very special occasion for Sanna. Today, I more often purchase desiccated cardamom seeds usually found in little bags at the supermarket, although I prefer the strength of the flavor of the seeds that I get from cardamom in the original pods. The bleached white cardamom pods are most familiar to Scandinavians. In many cuisines, such as Indian cooking, they use cardamom from green pods. In either case, the pods need to be opened up and the black seeds removed. That's what you measure. I crush these seeds in a coffee grinder that I reserve just for this purpose. Cardamom loses its flavor quickly after being ground. Therefore I never bother to buy the already-ground cardamom in jars.

** "Pearl sugar" looks like crushed sugar cubes and is available in Scandinavian markets.

Korppu

Traditionally, Finnish women baked coffee bread—like the pulla recipe above—on Saturdays. If there was bread left from the baking a week before, they sliced it and toasted it in the oven until it was crisp and dry to make "korppu." The dry toast kept well when it was stored in an airtight container, usually a glass jar with a screw-on lid. Korppu was eaten with coffee—often dunked into hot coffee to soften. I remember stacking korppu next to a cup of hot cocoa and dunking a piece at a time to soften and make it "squishy" and delicious. Because cinnamon is much cheaper than cardamom and readily available, the coffee bread and korppu often were flavored or coated with cinnamon sugar.

Korppu was so popular and such a good way to use day-old bread that it became one of the products of the Zinsmaster Baking Company in Duluth. The Zinsmaster Baking Company was founded in Duluth in 1913 as the Zinsmaster–Smith Bread Co. by Harry W. Zinsmaster and R. F. Smith. The small local enterprise grew to one of national importance. Additional Zinsmaster companies were located in St. Paul, Minneapolis, Hibbing, and Superior, Wisconsin. Recently, I received a gift of a bag of korppua from a cousin who lives in Floodwood. The Finns proudly call it "biscotti," and though that name is technically correct, as it is a twice-baked product, korppu bears no resemblance to the Italian classic.

My Maternal Grandparents

A Story of Famine, Fire, and Fear

My maternal grandfather, Joel Sakris Honkala, was the only one of five boys who didn't starve to death in the famine of the late 1800s in northern Finland. Because his family wanted a better life for him, they pooled their money and bought him passage to America when he was in his late teens. I don't know why, but he first went to Florida; perhaps others in his group were headed that way, too. The Grandpa Honkala I knew wore a rather floppy fedora, sometimes a bit askew, and by the time I was thirteen he had shrunk to my height. His arthritis caused him to limp and he was bowlegged. Through all of that, though, he was a smiling, affable character who loved his grandchildren.

Grandpa Honkala—who would give me the name of "Peetsi" or "Peachie"—was baffled by the modern names of his grandchildren. That's a fruit, he mused when he heard my name, Beatrice, which sounded like *peesti* to him, or "peach." Then came Lillian or "Liljan kukka," *kukka* being Finnish for "flower," and then Marion, or *marja*—a berry. All these names are a translation, mixing Finnish and English. When a cousin of mine was born who was named "Carol Jean," he exclaimed, "Karosine! Now I have heard it all!"

When Grandpa was younger and had just immigrated to Florida, he picked up a saxophone and I've heard did very well—so well that he earned enough money playing in a dance band that he could go back to Finland and marry my grandmother, Amanda Aurora Nevala Tassi, who was called "Ruusu," Rose.

Ruusu was a seamstress and owned a small dress shop in Kurikka, a village in the western part of Finland. The first two years after their marriage were difficult. She lost a child. Then my aunt Elma was born. They decided to sell the dress shop and all that was in it and use the money to leave Finland and go to America.

Joel undoubtedly had favorable things to say about America, and they prepared to leave—this time to go to Minnesota, where they heard they could get free land to build a farming life. They homesteaded in Brookston, about twenty-five miles west of Duluth, around the year 1910. They had a boy, Alfred, and in 1913, my mother, Esther, was born. Two years later, my aunt Helen was born. Grandpa built a nice, wood frame house, large for the area, that had both an upstairs and a downstairs for his wife and four children.

My mother, Esther Alma Honkala (Luoma), at three years in 1916.

The year 1918 had been hot and dry—the woods and fields were tinder-dry, and the crops hadn't done well. It is claimed that a spark from a coal-burning train combined with extremely dry conditions started the horrific fire that began in Cloquet, Minnesota, in October of that year and spread northward. Over 450 lives were lost, dozens of communities were destroyed, and hundreds of thousands of acres of woods burned. For people lost in a single day, it remains the worst natural disaster in the history of Minnesota. My grandparents and their family, including my five-year-old mother, were caught in the middle of it.

As the fire moved swiftly toward their farm, my grandfather Joel and his son, Alfred, lowered buckets into their well and used the water to wet the house and its surroundings. They turned the cows, the horses, and the pigs loose out of their barns. Ruusu hauled household belongings, including baked loaves of bread and canned goods, into the root cellar not far from the house. Joel kept dousing the house with the buckets of water.

Ruusu was known for being excitable, and in a frenzy as she saw the flames coming toward them and soon to engulf them all, she put my mother, Elma, Alfred, and Helen into a horse cart and took off at a gallop. To her dying day, my mother wondered where her mother thought she could escape to ahead of the flames. But the flames encircled them.

The horse was soon overcome, and the cart became mired in a creek bed. Ruusu, with Elma and Alfred, ran back to the house. My mother and her three-year-old sister, Helen, crawled under the seat. "But where are the little girls?" Grandpa Joel yelled. Ruusu said they were already dead in the cart.

"They are not dead!" Joel cried. With that he ran through the flames to the cart, put the girls, both of them singed and burned, over his shoulders, and brought them back to the house.

My mother, Esther, had the most burns of the two girls. Her arms were badly burned, as were her legs and thighs. Her skin grew back silky and patterned. Growing up, accustomed to the swirls and curls of the scars on my mother's arms, I thought that all mothers had "flowers on their arms." I would sit on her lap and trace the petals and leaves with my little fingers, and I thought her arms were beautiful. I don't think she wanted to scare me, but as I grew older she told me the story about the fire little by little.

After Grandpa had saved the girls, the winds changed and the farmhouse did not burn. All of the animals died except for one horse and its foal, which stood in the middle of a plowed field and were spared. Even when that horse grew old and lame, Grandpa couldn't bring himself to destroy it. My mother and father inherited the horse after they were married and it lived with them for many years.

After the fire died down around their farm, the Red Cross arrived. The fire had moved on toward Duluth—which made the Grand Rapids hospital, about fifty miles to the northwest, more accessible than Duluth's hospital, even though Duluth would have been about twenty-five miles closer. My mother and Helen were hospitalized, and Ruusu went along to assist the nursing staff. The hospital was teeming with burned and sick people.

In letters that my mother saved, Ruusu had written to Joel, telling of how lonesome she was and how badly Esther was burned, but how she didn't complain. Ruusu asked my grandfather questions like, "Did the bread survive the fire?" and "Was everything destroyed?" It was late October, winter was coming, and Joel had his hands full preparing as much as he could for the cold months to come.

After a painful month in the hospital, and to make matters even worse after the horrific fire, there came word of a rising influenza epidemic. The flu pandemic of 1918 affected five hundred million people across the world and killed three to five percent of the world's population.

One morning Grandpa Joel made his usual phone call to the hospital. He asked about the condition of his daughters. The answer was, "Your daughters are doing well, but your wife died last night." Ruusu, in the hospital taking care of her children, had taken ill and died. In some of her letters to Joel, she was asking for more warm underwear as she felt so chilled. I wonder how long she actually was ill. My mother told me she remembered seeing her mother's body, passing by, covered, on a gurney. "I don't know how, but I knew it—that my mother was dead."

Ruusu had, over the few years that she and Joel had lived in Brookston, seemingly befriended everyone. She was the first to be there when a baby was born, when somebody was sick, when anybody needed help. She was there with food, care, and concern. Ruusu was beloved by all. The news of her death shocked the township and the neighboring townships.

There was Joel, now desperately in need of help. Four children, two of them badly burned in the fire, the farm all but demolished, and winter coming on.

Brookston is on the northern edge of the Fond du Lac reservation. Finns and American Indians got along well. They had similar skills, similar problems, and similar resourceful mentalities. My mother as well as the whole family learned to speak Ojibwe. The Ojibwe in the area learned Finnish. They had a deep kinship. One of the Indian families offered to adopt my mother and her siblings after the horrible events. But, of course, Grandpa Joel would hear none of that.

Instead, he wrote for a Finnish "mail-order bride" who, he said, had to be able to cook and keep house. That was all he asked.

Helena Lindgren had taken chef's training in Helsinki so that she could be employed in New York City until she was called to be a mail-order bride. She was among the seven percent of Finns whose first language was Swedish. Helena accepted Joel's invitation and headed for Minnesota.

Helena owned a cookbook that was published in Helsinki in 1909 and was written in two languages, English on the one side and Finnish on the other. It was published especially for young women in cookery school. The dual-language book was highly convenient: someone who employed a Finnish-trained cook could read the English version of each recipe and, without communicating in Finnish herself, tell her employee what she wanted cooked.

This book is in my library now. I have enjoyed deciphering Helena's notes in the book and especially her additional recipes scribbled in the margins. It took me years to realize that "Zugar Gukis" was her phonetic rendering of "sugar cookies" and that "Bunsk Kaik" meant "sponge cake."

Grandmother's Sugar Cookies

Here is the recipe for "Zugar Gukis" as it reads in Helena's cookbook.

1 glass sugar	½ pound butter
1 pound flour	½ cup milk
1 egg	1 teaspoon soda

There are no directions for assembly. However, in my experimentation, the following recipe is close:

1 cup sugar	1 teaspoon baking soda
1 cup butter	½ cup buttermilk
1 egg	1 teaspoon vanilla
3 cups all-purpose flour	Extra sugar for shaping

Preheat the oven to 375°F. Cream the 1 cup sugar and butter until smooth. Add the egg and beat until light. Mix the flour and baking soda and add to the creamed mixture alternately with the buttermilk and vanilla, mixing until a stiff dough is formed.

Shape the dough into balls the size of walnuts and place 2 inches apart on a greased or parchment-covered cookie sheet. With the bottom of a water glass dipped first in water and then in sugar, stamp the cookies to flatten out to about 2½ to 3 inches. Bake about 10 minutes until light golden.

Makes about 4 dozen cookies

Life in Brookston, Minnesota, was a far cry from the relative luxury Helena had known in New York. It was November 1918, with winter coming, on a burned-out farm where she was called to replace the wife of somebody she did not know in the least. And Helena certainly came to realize that she was expected to fill the shoes of a woman who now was almost sainted in the community. Helena's kitchen became her castle, and nobody was allowed in—especially my mother and her sisters. Although Helena was an excellent cook, she was not a teacher and vehemently disliked my mother, saying (in Finnish), "I don't need a watchdog in my kitchen." My mother decided right there that her kids would learn how to cook and would always be welcome in her kitchen. Her experience made a lasting impression on my mother, and ultimately, on me.

To finish high school, my mom moved to Duluth, where she worked for

*Grandpa Joel
Sakris Honkala
and "stepmother"
Helena Lindgren
Honkala, mid-1940s.
My mother never
referred to Helena as
"mother" but always
as "stepmother."*

her room and board with a Jewish family by the name of Stern who would become lifelong family friends. She enrolled in Duluth's Central High School, an imposing, beautiful building that was built in 1892 of locally quarried sandstone.

Most everyone who has visited Duluth, even today, knows Old Central with its 230-foot clock tower that rises above the downtown, a Romanesque brownstone building modeled after the Allegheny Courthouse in Pittsburgh, Pennsylvania. The building's brownstone came from the Krause Quarry in Fond du Lac and other quarries along the Wisconsin south shore of Lake Superior. Today, when I drive through Duluth and see that building, thoughts of my mother come to mind.

Mom said her shoes never fit properly, and she told me she would kick them off under her desk. For this she was bullied and kids would throw her shoes down the hallway to embarrass her. Finally, in her junior year she couldn't take the harassment anymore and dropped out of school.

At the same time, my father, Ted, had left his home in Cedar Valley and was working at the Neil Bort Pie Company in Duluth. Neil Bort Pies were small handheld pies that had fillings of chocolate, lemon, apple, berries, and other fruits.

The two met at a dance at the "62 Hall" in Brookston. Mom had continued to work as a household assistant and cook for the Stern family in Duluth after dropping out of school. After dating for a short time, my mother and father were married on October 29, 1933, on his family's farm in Cedar Valley.

When Ted took Esther home to meet the Luoma family, his mother, Sanna, asked the critical question, "Are you a Laestadiolainen?," referring to a form of conservative Lutheran revivalism common at that time in Scandinavian countries, including Finland.

Although Sanna was steadfastly religious, she did not subscribe to the Laestadian philosophy. Rather, the family worshiped about once a month in a small Lutheran church in Cedar Valley. In the winter they held their "services" in homes because the little church building had only a woodstove in the middle of the floor for heat and to this day has only a two-hole outhouse, about twenty feet from the structure, and no place to park either cars or horses and wagons.

Mom replied that no, she wasn't. And with that, she was approved to join the family.

First Names First

My parents had no honeymoon, but according to country tradition, Ted's brothers tied cowbells to the springs of the bed—quite a bit different from the usual painted and decorated getaway car that Dick and I would later have at our wedding.

I was conceived and born in the same bed, and in the same house my father, Isä, had been born in twenty-five years earlier. I was born on July 22, 1934. As I like to say, on the day I was born, my life changed. For some unknown reason, my father insisted on naming me "Beatrice," which was an unusual name for a Finn to choose. After all, the Finns don't even use the letter *b* in their language. The letter *b* is pronounced somewhere between a *b* and a *p*.

You might ask, "What difference does that little fact make?"

When my grandfather came to visit—the same day I was born—he asked, "What is the baby's name?"

My mother replied, "Beatrice."

"*Peetsis*? That's no human name, that's a fruit!" he said in Finnish.

The name stuck. From that day on, my name was "Peachie" or "Peaches." I was known to Finns as "Pikku Peetsi" or "Little Peachie."

This name "problem" could have been solved if I'd followed my mother's advice the day I started first grade in Floodwood. As I took off for school in the big yellow bus, Mummy told me, "Now remember that your name is *Beatrice*. You don't want to be stuck with a nickname all your life!"

I settled in to my classroom with thirty-four classmates. Miss Pappanen named all of the students in the class. Then she said, "Hmm, we have two Beatrices—how are we going to tell them apart?"

I waved my hand enthusiastically, "I know, I know! You can call me Peaches!" So, Peaches it was from that point on in my life. Even my elementary school report card named me as "Peaches Luoma." It just seemed so very normal.

The other Beatrice and I bonded immediately. She later became known as "Bea," but I remained Peaches or Peachie.

To this day I have trouble introducing myself as Bea. It is like stealing my best friend's name.

At eighteen months, I was already "Peaches" to my family.

Nine months old, April 1935. One of the kitchen chairs was brought outside for this photograph.

My mother said I was a hungry baby. There was always homemade rye bread in the house and when I was just a few months old, she would leave a slice of buttered bread next to my crib. When I woke at night, I'd find it, sit up, and eat every last crumb; then I'd crawl back under the covers, satisfied. A friend once told Mummy that she was "spoiling" me and that no child had to be fed in the middle of the night. My mother didn't have the heart to break me of the habit of midnight eating with no warning, so she decided to wean me off it. One night she put a crust of dry, unbuttered, hard bread next to my crib, thinking I'd reject it. When I woke for my usual snack, I took that crust and gnawed and chewed away at it until it was finished. Then I went back to sleep. This made her sad. She continued with the slice of buttered bread. I don't remember how long. To this day when I'm hungry, all it takes is a slice of whole grain Finnish rye bread to satisfy me.

The Finnish rye bread that was a staple in our house is a simple bread, made with milk or water, coarse rye flour, white bread flour, a little salt, a little sugar, and yeast. My mother made it in large batches, once or twice a week, depending on how many extra mouths there would be at the table. If somebody showed up at the doorstep around mealtime, they were always invited to sit down and share a meal. Usually the menu consisted of Finnish rye bread (you'll find that recipe later in the book) and a strange-sounding stew called "mojakka" that is really a hearty beef (or in our case, venison) stew with potatoes, onions, and rutabagas. The stew is simmered over low heat until the meat and vegetables are "falling apart" tender. Nobody really knows where the name comes from. It isn't known in Finland, nor does it appear in any dictionary. Mojakka can be made with a meat base, or it can be made with fish. It got so that whenever we had leftover meat on hand, we would turn it into mojakka.

Finnish-Style Mojakka

This stew (pronounced moy-yah-kah) is known only to American Finns, largely in the Upper Midwest, and can be made with any kind of meat. We most often made it with venison. The vegetables vary, but we always used root vegetables—whatever we had on hand.

3 pounds boneless beef or venison cubes, or leftover roast, trimmed and
    cut up
2 tablespoons butter, lard, or oil
4½ to 5 cups water
1 onion, thinly sliced
2 teaspoons salt
½ teaspoon ground black pepper
½ teaspoon whole allspice (optional)
2 cups chopped carrots, rutabaga, turnips, parsnips, or other root vegetables
4 potatoes, peeled and cubed
2 tablespoons all-purpose flour

In a large pot over medium high heat, brown the meat on all sides in the butter. (If using leftover roast, you can skip this step.) Add 4 cups of the water and bring to a boil. Add the onion, salt, ground black pepper, and optional allspice. Reduce heat to low and simmer for one hour or until the meat is "falling apart" tender.

Add the carrots and/or other root vegetables and potatoes and simmer for another 1½ hours. Mix the flour and remaining ½ cup water in a separate small bowl, forming a thin paste. Add this to the soup, stirring well and simmer for 15 more minutes.

Makes 8–10 servings

Growing Up on a Farm in Northern Minnesota

In the poem "Ulysses," Alfred, Lord Tennyson said, "I am a part of all that I have met." This statement implies that all encounters, whether positive or negative, are a part of our psyche. It might even mean that we should avoid the negative. In my mind anyway, negative encounters have a reflective reaction within us that brings out positive images.

The farmerly tasks that were assigned to me at a tender age would be unthinkable today. I shoveled cow manure in the barn, raked poop in the chicken coop. I learned to drive the "joker"—a converted Ford, I think it was a Model A, without floorboards, a cab, or fenders. I was twelve years old at the time. We used the joker to pull the hay mower, hay rake, and wagon. When I was sixteen, my parents took a road trip to Oregon to visit my aunt Elma. Two of my sisters went along on the trip, and the rest of the kids were left behind for me to care for along with the routine farm chores, with which I was very familiar by then. There were cows to be fed and milked morning and evening; the milk had to be strained, chilled, and stored in ten-gallon containers, then lifted into a cooling tank to chill before the milkman came to pick them up. The chickens had to be cared for, eggs gathered, and the garden vegetables picked, cleaned, and put away.

The cows were my confidants. I knew each one by name and personality. I was feeding and milking them at the age of ten. By the time the sun came up in the winter, I had milked my share, gulped down a bowl of hot oatmeal, changed from barn clothes to school clothes, grabbed my books and homework, and torn down the quarter-mile road to catch the big, yellow school bus at the corner of what is now named Benson Road.

Many years later, I wondered if my classmates could smell barn on me in school. I asked that question just last week. The reply? "We all smelled like barn!"

We had round, galvanized tubs that usually were used in the sauna building when Mummy washed clothes. In the summertime on hot days, we would fill the tubs with water and set them out to be heated by the sun. We would run out and swish the water around until we determined that the water was

Leonard and I enjoy a summertime "swim," while Isä drives the Ferguson tractor in the field behind us.

warm enough to go "swimming." I would wear a sunsuit and my younger brother Leonard would wear a pair of shorts. Or nothing. We never worried about sunburn and I don't recall being burned.

When the Rural Electric Association moved into our area in 1940, my parents were the first to sign up. I was six years old at the time. A Westinghouse stove and refrigerator found a place in the kitchen. Even though we could now cook anything with the turn of a knob, we still fired up the woodstove for baking crusty rye bread and for its "coziness." I still believe you can't get the same kind of crust on bread as you can when it is baked in a wood-fired oven.

The Westinghouse refrigerator had smooth rounded corners and hummed away in the kitchen; it took the place of the old oak icebox and was most exciting. The refrigerator came with a cookbook and directions for making ice cream. We always had plenty of milk, cream, and eggs on hand, and in the summertime I could add fresh berries from the woods and fields. I would skim the cream that rose to the top of the ten-gallon containers and mix and churn the cream into ice cream and butter.

It was in about the fourth grade, when we were asked to write what was on our minds, that I truly discovered the joy of writing. From that day on, whenever we were told that part of the curriculum for whatever class we were taking was to write an essay, it excited me. My classmates groaned. This was the beginning of my quest to learn how to write, and that hasn't been easy. My language was peppered with Finnish words and though I was good at spelling, I wasn't sure of my grammar. I loved to do research in the library at school, no matter what the topic.

Further, all my routine tasks around the farm gave me ample time to dream about writing. I was too self-conscious to tell anybody, so I wrote secret stories and hid them. My parents gave me a used black Smith Corona typewriter one year for Christmas, and it became my prized possession. I could hack out stories and when I was brave enough, I sent them, secretly, to magazines like *Calling All Girls* and *Seventeen.* I collected a pile of rejection slips.

Much as I loved to cook, I hated the mandatory home economics classes at school. They were nothing new to me. The home economics teacher was short, fat, always wore black dresses, and had dandruff on her shoulders. The classes she taught were a series of endless repetition. Biscuits, muffins, cocoa brownies, and tiring talks about aprons, tying one's hair back, and washing hands. I wanted more. I wanted to write and I wanted to explore the traditional foods of the world. At the time I felt that I didn't know enough about anything to actually write about anything. I was a sponge ready to learn, and in addition I had an imagination that had plenty of freedom to roam.

Mr. Riley, the science teacher, was a true inspiration. He was a tough disciplinarian, and the physics and chemistry he taught all made sense to me. I learned the difference between baking soda and baking powder in chemistry class. Soda is a base that reacts with an acid to make a cake rise. Baking powder, on the other hand, has both a base and an acid in its makeup, and all it requires is a liquid to spur the action. I figured the reason that we used one combination or another was merely a matter of taste.

English classes weren't quite as easy to figure out, although I did enjoy reading the classics that were assigned to us. I couldn't relate to the characters because I thought they lived in such exotic places. I couldn't picture the March girls in *Little Women* in barn clothes! But still I thought the farm we lived on was the most beautiful place in the world.

I would walk through the woods and over the fields and hold my fingers to shape a square and imagine a "calendar picture" right in front of me. I'd name the scenes for the topic and season. It was many years later that I had a camera of my own, and when I got it, I was always behind it—so I was in the pictures only in spirit. It has always been fascinating to me to ponder the idea of inherited traits. Today with DNA testing I may learn the answers to many questions I have about my heritage. Following that thinking, we are also made up of our ancestors' personalities, whether we knew them personally or not. I have traced back certain traits to my grandparents and note their qualities in myself and my brothers and sisters. That is why I know that the stories about all of my grandparents are important. I thank God for their gifts and their strengths and weaknesses.

In northern Minnesota, a small farm in the mid-1900s required multiple incomes to survive. Springtime brought outside chores. There was the preparation of the fields for planting potatoes, wheat, and oats as well as plowing the "kitchen" garden. There were newborn calves to be nursed and cows with large, heavy bags to be milked twice a day.

We had to wean calves as soon as possible so that they would not be dependent on their mothers' milk. To do that, we had to teach the newborn calf to drink milk from a pail. Baby calves have an instinct to suck, so we had to let the calf suck our fingers as we gradually immersed our hand into the warm, sweet-smelling, frothy milk. There is a special aroma to the colostrum milk—it was sweet, a deep yellow, and a bit sticky. Once the calf learned to drink from a pail, we switched the feeding to a mixture of powdered milk and water and no longer had to pretend our fingers were nipples.

I have always loved the sights, sounds, and smells of springtime. The first sign was always from the song sparrows, which would sing their songs early in the morning, going from an A down to a D many octaves higher than I can identify on the piano. Sometimes it is just a lilting A–D and sometimes an A–DD, and I would listen for the answer from somewhere. I have always wondered what these birds were saying to each other. "Stay out of my territory"? Or "Welcome to my territory"? Then there is the sweet aroma in the air as the evergreens would awaken and the poplar trees started circulating their juices and the buds that eventually burst into leaves started to get sticky. There would be a white weblike film on the ground that needed to be raked away so that the tender grass could burst into life.

The chill in the springtime air, the slight crunch of the early-morning frozen mud on the driveway that slowly softened as the sun rose high enough to bake the surface dry by noon. These are the delights of spring, I'd think—a sure sign that the freezing cold of winter is behind. Springtime, I have always thought, holds such promise.

Salt Cake

By the time I was about five years old, I had already discovered that it was far more pleasurable to satisfy the wishes of my parents than to rebel. Maybe it was because my mother had lost her own mother at the age of five and grew up under the scolding hand of her stepmother that I wanted to please her. She must have told me stories about how she was physically and mentally abused, though I don't recall too much because the stories were so gradually revealed. The upshot of them, though, was that I carried the vision of the wicked stepmother in my mind. My mom would tell me more about her early childhood in bits and pieces much later.

She always referred to "Stepmother" when she talked about the woman who had replaced her mother after her untimely death. "Stepmother never let us into the kitchen," she would say. "So, I want my kids to know how to cook."

When she said I needed to learn how to bake a cake, I agreed. I was five years old. She took out the big tan crockery mixing bowl with blue stripes around the outside, the wooden spoon, and the essential ingredients: butter, sugar, eggs, salt, baking powder, flour, vanilla, and milk.

The woodstove had been fired up so that the gauge on the front of the oven read 350°F. It was January and although it was freezing outside, the kitchen was cozy and the stove was always hot and ready for baking. We were not yet powered for electricity.

I attentively watched and made mental notes of what the batter looked like. She scooped an egg-sized sphere of butter and slapped it into the bowl. "About a half cup is right," she said. Then she poked the butter with the tip of the wooden spoon, making indentations that looked like so many commas in a row. This was to soften the butter, she said.

Then she added sugar in twice the measure of the butter, about a cup, and stirred it until it was all creamy. Next she added eggs, two of them, stirring really fast so that the liquid of the eggs was whipped into the butter mixture. She went on to mix in the flour and baking powder, and explained that one teaspoon of baking powder to one cup of flour was the best proportion. Vanilla for flavor and enough milk to make a smooth, pourable batter—and the cake was ready for the baking pan.

"Taste it," she said. "If it tastes flat—add a pinch of salt." We did, and

Mummy's Simple White Cake

½ cup (1 stick) butter, softened
1 cup sugar
2 eggs
2 cups all-purpose flour
2 teaspoons baking powder
½ teaspoon salt
1 cup milk
1 teaspoon vanilla

Preheat the oven to 350°F. Butter a 9- x 13-inch cake pan.
In a large mixing bowl, cream the butter with the sugar. Add the eggs and beat until fluffy. Stir the flour, baking powder, and salt together and add to the creamed mixture alternately with the milk. Stir in the vanilla. Beat until light and fluffy. Spread evenly into the cake pan.
Bake for 25 to 30 minutes until the center springs back when touched or until a toothpick inserted into the center of the cake comes out clean and dry. The cake is perfect simply cut into squares, but sometimes we sprinkled cinnamon sugar over the top.

mixed a little salt in. Then we scraped the batter into the buttered pan and stuck it into the oven to bake, until a straw plucked from the corn broom and stuck into the center of the cake came out clean and dry.

It was a couple of weeks later and my mother was in labor, not an uncommon occurrence (there eventually were ten of us children). This was the day my sister Lillian was born. Dr. Van (Floodwood's resident physician) and my father were in the bedroom with my mother. I wasn't allowed into the room. The kitchen stove was fired up because they needed boiling water to sterilize the doctor's equipment. My job was to open the side lid of the woodstove and add a piece of firewood every fifteen minutes or so.

It was then I decided to bake a cake for Mummy.

I took out the bowl and spoon and tried to remember all the ingredients. I hadn't started school yet and hadn't learned to write, so I had to remember the recipe. I mixed the batter as I had been instructed and, last of all, tasted it. It was flat, so I added a pinch of salt. Still flat. I added another pinch of salt. Still flat. Finally I was tossing handfuls of salt into the batter, and it didn't seem to be helping at all. The batter looked good, though, and I poured it into the pan and put it into the oven. Pondering what could have been wrong when the cake was half-baked, I realized that I had forgotten the sugar. This was a lesson that served me well the rest of my life. Always taste to see what's missing!

The cake turned out golden and beautiful. It looked delicious! I proudly served my mother a square of the freshly baked cake while she was lying in bed after having given birth to Lillian. She didn't say anything about it being salty. She only said that it looked beautiful.

Many years later she admitted that the cake I had made was so salty it made her tongue curl. That was Mummy—always encouraging and always looking for the best.

There Were Ten of Us

I am very fortunate to have grown up in a home full of brothers and sisters. To understand who I am, you must understand a little about them, too, and our lives together on the farm in Floodwood.

I was two years old when my brother Leonard, the second oldest in our family, was born. By the time he was a year old or so, my parents recognized that there was something wrong. Deafness runs in the Luoma family, but they didn't want to believe Leonard might be affected. My dad had a brother named Walter who was born deaf and died early in life from tuberculosis. They didn't want to believe that this trait would be inherited. I recall my parents taking Leonard to every doctor they could, and it was a doctor in Rush City who finally gave them the news. Leonard was born deaf with weak (or no) audio nerves. I remember Mummy weeping. He appeared to be a perfect baby with strong bones and "all ten toes" as the old saying goes.

As a baby and as a toddler, Leonard noticed everything and was super-active and fearless. When he was about four years old, our father started to build a new barn for the farm. The barn stood thirty-two feet high and forty feet long with the typical rounded roof. Near the top of the roof during construction, there was a long and narrow plank that ran from the front to the back of the barn's frame.

To the horror of my parents, Leonard climbed fearlessly to that narrow plank and ran back and forth from the front to the back again and again, some thirty feet off the ground. You couldn't yell at him because, of course, he couldn't hear. I don't know how they got him down to the ground; all I know is that my six-year-old heart was beating like a drum. Finally, they did get him down, but there was no way to explain the danger to him and the fright we all felt.

Two years later Leonard was enrolled in the Minnesota School for the Deaf in Faribault, now called the Minnesota State Academy for the Deaf. It was a sad and happy situation for the family. We so looked forward to Christmas and summer holidays, anxious to see how much language he had learned. It was always a sad day when Leonard had to return to school, but we were thankful and happy that he had such a great opportunity to learn communication skills along with the traditional curriculum that we had

Leonard and I at the farmhouse, ages two and three, in 1937.

in school. This was in the days before American Sign Language was used. At home, we learned to spell-sign words, so we could communicate with Leonard in a very rudimentary but convenient manner. Today, we all would have learned ASL.

Faribault was known for producing blue cheese. The students at the Minnesota School for the Deaf were taken on regular field trips to the blue cheese caves and obviously were treated to samples. These samples developed a taste for blue cheese in most of the students, including my brother. I especially remember his delight when we'd buy a square of Treasure Cave blue cheese. Later, the company that bought the caves moved their production to a facility in another state and closed down Treasure Cave in the Faribault area in the 1990s. To this day, one of the best gifts I can give Leonard is a hunk of blue cheese.

My sister Marion came next. She and I did a lot together growing up and were always the best of friends—from peeling "popple" (our name for poplar trees) in the woods, to caring for the chickens, to barn work. We made up stories to entertain each other while picking berries, weeding the garden, and doing chores. Even today, Marion and I have a special "sisterly" connection. We taught each other to be terrible shoppers. On our trips to Duluth, we lusted over items in Woolworth's, Kresge's, or the Ben Franklin stores where we could buy a little vial of Blue Waltz Perfume for twelve cents or a little fake watch with hands that were permanently fixed so that the face read ten minutes to the hour or twenty minutes after. We would look at each other and ask the question, "Can I live without it?" Of course, the answer was always yes, so we didn't spend any of our hard-earned money to buy anything. Even today, we follow the "Can I live without it?" rule.

Lillian, my parents' fourth child, was born on the day that I created the Salt Cake. Lil was always popular in high school, an athlete, cheerleader, adventurer—she was all around a lot of fun to be with. Her cooking adventures were not as serious as mine, but what I learned from her early experiences has given me a chuckle. Directions for a cake recipe said to cream the butter and sugar together. Noticing there was no cream in the ingredient list, Lil was puzzled, so she just dumped in some cream. I never did find out how that cake turned out.

When Lil was born, I had begged my parents to name her Betty Mae after a beautiful dark-haired doll I had gotten as a Christmas present that came prenamed "Betty Mae." My doll had dark curly hair and a pretty face. Mummy and Isä promised that the "next" baby girl would be called Betty Mae.

Betty Mae has since been questioned as to why a "northern girl" like her has such a "southern" name. But so it was. Betty Mae was born eighteen months after Lillian. She is the only one of us six girls who has dark hair! Betty Mae and Lillian were pals all through school; both of them were cheerleaders and shared friendships. Betty Mae went on to become a home economist.

Eugene, the sixth one to join the family, was the second son of the family after a string of girls, and I am sure his arrival delighted my father. He now had another son to whom he could pass on the resourcefulness required for country living. Eugene was quick and wily and learned his lessons well. He and Rudy (the next in line) would figure out all kinds of things, from ways to trap fish in the St. Louis River to outsmarting the game warden when they trapped weasels in the wintertime.

Eugene, always thinking, has invented so many things we can't keep up with him. One of his most successful gadgets is the Zip-It, a simple little tool you can use to unclog drains. When his long-haired daughter (all girls seem to have long hair these days) was at home, clogged drains were a regularity. So Eugene took a plastic strip (the kind that are used to secure boxes during shipping), cut notches on the sides, and used that to pull the stuff out of the drain.

Next came my brother Rudy—and seemingly always with mischief on their minds, Rudy and his older brother Eugene were inseparable. Only eighteen months apart, they did everything together, even after both of them grew up and got married. In this photo they look like lonely little kids—however, they probably had devised some plan and were about to head out to do it. It was Eugene with the ideas, and Rudy who would carry them to fruition.

Years later, Alvin, the fourth boy, was born into the family. Eugene and Rudy were admonished by Mummy and Isä to always include Alvin in their activities. Considering him a nuisance, one day they put Alvin into a gunnysack and hung him from a birch tree in the woods. Later, at the dinner table, Mummy noticed that Alvin was missing. "Where is Alvin?"

Rudy and Eugene guiltily glanced at each other, and one of them said, "Oh, we forgot! We hung him in a gunnysack in a tree!"

My brothers Rudy and Eugene on the front steps of our farmhouse in 1947, when Eugene was four years old and Rudy was almost three.

When I asked Alvin how he managed to spend all that time hung in a tree, he replied that he just fell asleep, crying, but knew somebody would come and get him. The mosquitoes, he recalls, were terrible as they bit right through the burlap gunnysack.

Even as grown-ups, Rudy and Eugene traveled together, worked on home projects together, devised schemes together, planned their hunting shack, and spent time there thinking of projects, solving problems, and telling jokes. After Eugene developed muscular dystrophy, Rudy became his right-hand man. He was always there ready to help out.

Of the ten of us, Rudy, the seventh child, was the most unlikely one to leave us first. He was only sixty-three, the tallest, and probably the fittest of us all. He was hit by a massive heart attack on a sunny December morning while drinking coffee and reading the newspaper.

The last time they were together, Rudy was laid out on a gurney in the ER and Eugene, devastated, sat in his motorized scooter. What was he going to do now? "Rudy's gone" was a hard reality to comprehend for us all. We loved him so much.

My sister Nancy was born with a motherly instinct. When I was in college and dating Dick, Nancy was in fourth or fifth grade and Mummy was pregnant again, embarrassingly for the tenth time. Nancy had been sworn to secrecy, as Mom was hesitant to announce to the world that there would be one more Luoma on the planet.

The complication was that Isä had had his tubes tied and was supposed to be sterile. This threw my parents into a terrible quandary. Isä accused Mummy of sleeping with the milkman, the veterinarian, almost every man who came to the farm. She was devastated, as she had never done such a thing. She insisted that he was the father of her unborn child.

Isä later went to his doctor to get himself checked out—and sure enough, the tubes had come untied!

This all happened the year Dick and I became engaged. Nancy was so excited about the prospect of a new baby in the house, she could hardly contain herself.

As news in small towns tends to spread, eventually, Nancy's friend on the school bus asked her, "Is your mother going to have another baby?"

Nancy, wanting to tell her friend that there would, indeed, be a baby in the house, blurted out, "No, but Peachie is!"

Of course, this news was bound to spread even more quickly. When Mummy heard about it, she got on the party line (our country telephones at the time were all hooked to a single party line) and called her sister Helen, talking about the new baby she was about to have. She could hear the *click,*

click, click as the neighbors picked up their phones. The news was out—and I was off the hook!

Alvin, like his brothers, is a guy with many talents. A horticulturist at heart, he spent his working days for Minnesota Power as a lineman. When I was a student at the university and home for a weekend, Alvin (in grade school at the time) would wake me up enthusiastically on Saturday morning to show me plants he had grown. They were long, skinny things that in the winter, with a dearth of sunshine, grew leggy and thin. But he was so excited to show me his latest.

He took the harassment from his older brothers in stride. When they accused him of being really, really dumb, they asked him smartly, "How much is one and one?" Alvin answered, "Two!"

"How much is two and two?"

With eyes smartly closed, pursed lips, he answered, "Two and two is easy!"

One summer, Eugene and Rudy decided they would try to raise enough money to buy a motorbike by doing chores. Of course, with Alvin being so young, he was not capable of doing as many things as the older boys, but he did contribute what bits he could and their goal was eventually accomplished. They bought a used motorbike.

The older brothers, having raised most of the money for the bike, told Alvin, "The only thing you earned was the air in the tires!"

Alvin's answer, "Well, then, I'll take my air back!"

Dawn, the infamous number ten in the family, wasn't going to be left behind! A straight A student and an accomplished flutist, she went on to the University of Minnesota to become an architect. Her designs are creative—in fact, she designed the home we now live in. But that's not all. She tried her hand at retail children's clothing, then gave up the idea. Dawn is now the family expert on the Minnesota Twins, and she follows baseball religiously!

It turned out that Dawn and our daughter, Cathy, were separated in age by only two years. So, Dawn was "Auntie Dawn" to Cathy—a position that seemed hilarious as they made mud pies together.

Being Finnish

We were Finns and almost everybody else we knew was a *toiskielinen*, or a person of "another tongue."

Our closest neighbor, a quarter mile away from where our driveway started, lived on the corner where we caught the school bus. It wasn't a corner at all. It's the dead end of what is now called Benson Road, named after the people who bought the farm from my parents in 1962.

Our neighbors were a combination of one hundred percent Norwegian and German (or Pennsylvania Dutch) and Mennonites. Instead of going to the Lutheran church that we attended, the neighbors went to the Bible Chapel in Floodwood—an amalgamation of various fundamental groups in the area. They often alluded to the fact that we were condemned to hell if we didn't repent and be saved. This was an idea that puzzled me.

We thought they were nice people, but later we found out that the neighbor kids had been instructed not to associate with our family because we were heathens, and I suppose they thought our evil ways would rub off on them. Or something like that. It was a funny thing, but they never hesitated to ask for help when they needed it.

The mother of our closest neighbor family, the Mennonites, almost always wore a "huivi" wrapped around her head. Or, that's what we Finns called the cotton scarf that she wrapped tightly and knotted just below her hairline on the back of her head. On very rare occasions, she would appear with her long, dark hair tightly rolled up on a rag to make a shiny, smooth rope around her head. It was the style, but they did not want to be too worldly and stylish.

Our neighbors lived a different way from our Finnish standards. Their house was cluttered and had a musty smell, and they allowed cats to run across the big round kitchen table.

I remember once when I was offered a slice of freshly baked bread. The cat had just been shooed off the table, and the bread placed down just where the cat had sat. I can't remember if I was polite enough to eat that slice of bread, or if I had just remembered something I needed to do and took off quickly.

Most of the time we had to run the quarter mile to catch the school bus, but sometimes in the winter when the bus was late, usually due to bad weather, they would invite us into their house to stay warm. I never really liked it because their house smelled funny, and if they offered me something to eat, like a cookie, I couldn't touch it. I could just picture a cat licking the cookie dough spoon.

For their summertime bathing, they had a big white bathtub outside under the willow trees that was enclosed in a tent. I don't know what they did in the winter. Our family always bathed in our sauna on Saturday night, fall, winter, spring, or summer, and though my mother invited the neighbors to sauna, they never came.

"You can't get clean in a bathtub," my father used to say. "You've got to take a sauna and then scrub yourself all over!" You had to sweat and when you sweated, you could rub off white stuff from your skin. That's when you were really clean.

"Sauna" was a ritual. We bathed every Saturday night and the night before any important holiday, like Christmas, or if important company came to visit. In the summertime, we had sauna almost every night during haymaking season, just to cool off and wash away bits of itchy dried hay that stuck to our sweaty skin.

The sauna was a separate building away from the house. It had two rooms: the first was the dual-purpose dressing room and laundry where my mother washed clothes on Mondays using a wringer washer. After churning everything in hot soapy water, she fed the clothes through the handwringer into galvanized rinse tubs. Then, after rinsing the clothes by hand, she would again feed them through the wringer, turning them into long, flat, twelve-inch-wide ribbons that had to be shaken out and hung on an outside clothesline to dry. In the winter, the wet laundry would freeze into stiff boards, and by evaporation got almost dry.

We brought the semidry laundry into the house, fired up the wood-burning stove, and placed sadirons on the top to heat up. Sadirons—or sad irons, the name coming from an Old English word meaning "solid"—were used in the days before we had electricity. They were thick slabs of cast iron, delta-shaped and with a handle, heated on top of the stove. These were also called flatirons. After we had electricity, we switched to electric irons.

In our sauna building there was a long, homemade bench in the dressing room that was also used for the laundry. The bench spanned the full length of the room, and that's where we would sit to cool off after soaking in the belching steam that we created in the hot room, or steam room, of the sauna. The floor of the dressing room was always covered with clean handwoven rag rugs.

Those rugs were all woven by my aunt Martha, who had a loom. Martha used strips of fabric from old clothing. To make the colorful balls, we cut old clothing, sheets, and anything that had outworn its initial use into 1½-inch strips. We would wrap the strips into balls and when we had a basketful, we would transport them to Martha, who then wove them into rugs. It was always fun to try and recognize the patterns in the rugs that came from our old clothes.

The steam room of the sauna had a stove fashioned out of an oil barrel that had pipes through it and that circled into another oil barrel that was made to hold and heat water. The barrel stove was covered with rocks that would heat up from the wood fire. To fill the water barrel, we carried pails of water, pumped from the well near the house. As the water circulated in the pipe through the fire, it would heat up. This took a long time—at least three hours—so we had to have a good, hot fire going.

The steam room had a concrete floor with a drain that was covered with a wooden platform and shelves that we called "lavas" on three different levels. The top level was always the hottest, especially when you threw a ladleful of water onto the hot rocks. This phenomenon is called *löyly*. Because of the steam, only when kids were big enough were they allowed to climb to the top level. We would watch the temperature on the thermometer on the wall go down when the water we threw on the rocks burst into steam, making us feel hotter and hotter.

We all took turns taking our sauna baths. First, we'd bathe the "little kids," and then the girls went in together and then the boys took their sauna together. We girls never went in with the boys, nor did women bathe with men. The only exception was that husbands and wives usually bathed together.

As we steamed, we'd rub ourselves with Jergen's soap and wet washcloths.

Little brother Alvin at three years old, in the sauna in his tub on the "lava."

I loved the floral aroma of the soap, especially if it was a "new" bar, just un-wrapped. We each had our own pan of water for bathing. Last of all, we would dump ladles of cold water over ourselves to cool and rinse ourselves. Then, we'd go into the dressing room to dry off and put on nightclothes, and run into the house to read the funny papers (the Sunday paper always arrived on Saturday in the mail in Floodwood). Then we'd drink bottles of orange, straw-berry, or cream soda that Isä brought from town as our Saturday night treat.

I loved the "Saturday night" feeling because we had spent the day scrub-bing the floors, baking bread or a cake, and sometimes some cookies. Sat-urday was the day to wash the bedsheets and the clean aroma from drying outside was delicious.

Sunday was the day of rest, although it was only once a month that we had worship services—at Uncle Frank's house. But that is another story.

Thin Finnish Pancakes (Lattyja)

Sometimes we call these "flapjacks"—they are very thin pancakes that are quick to make and perfect for a quick breakfast or simple supper. For a dessert, they can be served with berries and whipped cream. Sometimes I use buttermilk in place of milk—that would make them "buttermilk pancakes." The batter can be made the night before, then refrigerated. If it thickens beyond being pourable, just add more milk or buttermilk.

2 eggs
1 teaspoon sugar
½ teaspoon salt
1 cup milk or buttermilk
2 tablespoons melted butter
1 cup all-purpose flour
Butter for the pan

In a medium-sized bowl, whisk the eggs, sugar, and salt together. Add the milk, butter, and flour and whisk until smooth. Cover and let stand for 1 hour before cooking the pancakes.

Heat a heavy skillet or a Scandinavian-style pancake pan, and brush with butter. Spoon the batter into the pan, using no more than 2 tablespoons of the mixture at a time. Cook on both sides until golden and serve hot.

Makes about 20

Sunday Services at Uncle Frank's

Even though there were two Lutheran churches in Floodwood, we went to Finnish Lutheran services once a month in Cedar Valley, about twelve miles away. During the cold months we'd usually go to Uncle Frank's farm, where the traveling *pappi* (pastor) would lead the service. I was baptized at Uncle Frank's, as were my brothers and sisters. The baptisms were always at the service soonest after our birth.

Uncle Frank's house was built in the same plan as the old country farmhouses in Finland. You entered a small foyer with a painted floor where one could hang jackets and deposit muddy boots before entering the *tupa*, a large multipurpose kitchen/great room. The tupa had a woodstove and a trestle table, and in the expansive center of the room were a half dozen long wooden benches, all covered with clean and colorful home-woven rag rugs. The room also had a sink that included the convenience of a water pump on its left side. For hot water, you would pump water into a pail and transfer it to a boiler on the woodstove. This was a very modern kitchen in the 1930s and 1940s.

The aroma of boiled coffee and coffee bread, along with the smoke of the woodstove mixed with a kind of sweet "old house" smell, permeated the air. The combination hung on my clothes like incense even after we were home. If I were blindfolded when Uncle Frank and Aunt Mayme came over to visit, I could have identified them just by their smell.

When a service at Uncle Frank's started, we all sat quietly on the benches. I learned certain phrases in Finnish: "Isän ja pojan ja pyhä hengeen nimeen. Amen" (In the name of the Father and the Son and the Holy Spirit. Amen).

Psalms were sung in Finnish. I could sing by following along in the little book of psalms because Finnish is pronounced exactly the way it is written, but I couldn't understand a word of the service itself except for *Jumala,* which I knew was the word for God, and *Jeesus* (pronounced "yeesus") for Jesus.

Pastor Villen, looking very tall against the seven-foot-high ceiling, would launch into his sermon. Whenever I heard this phrase "Tosisesti, tosisesti, minä sanon teille" (Truly, truly, I say onto you), I knew he was quoting Jesus.

I waited for the final "Amen." That's when the adults would gather around the table for coffee, and us kids would take off, chasing after one another.

We'd play tag and kick the can and hide-and-seek and another game called "anti aye over" where we tossed a ball over the milk shed. My pretty voile dress with the buttons that looked like lingonberries soon hung limply from my shoulders as I'd have lost the belt. One pigtail would come undone, and my white stockings soon had black feet. My shoes were always too small, so I'd have kicked them off. Sweaty and rumpled, we'd finally be invited to the table for nectar (made from a syrup the traveling Rawleigh man sold) and, with it, squares of plain white cake.

On the way home, exhausted, we'd fall asleep in the backseat of the 1939 Packard that my dad felt very lucky to have been able to buy used. It was wartime and they weren't producing cars. I don't remember the important details of the car, such as whether it was the last of the V12s that Packard produced—all I remember are the sleek rounded lines, the black running boards, and a cushy backseat that could fit all five of us kids at the time.

Summers on the Farm

Summers on the farm in Floodwood started out with the peeling of "popple," or poplar trees. Between seasons, income had to be supplemented. For Isä, the opportunity came from the forest. Finns have a lumberjack heritage, and our woods were filled with mature poplar trees, which with the help of hired men Isä cut down in the early spring.

When school was out, my sister Marion, brother Leonard, and I were hired to remove the outer bark from the freshly cut logs. We were paid by the log.

We would tramp into the woods behind the barn and pasture and settle ourselves in the thicket of hazelnut bushes where the pile of eight-foot logs waited for us. Isä and his team of men would cut the trees from farther in the woods, load them onto skids—a sort of sled—and pull loads to us using the Ferguson tractor that had metal wheels with lugs so that it could be driven through a swamp.

The three of us spent many sweaty weeks in June with sharpened pieces of iron, stripping off the juicy exterior skin from the logs. The iron was made from metal that had been part of an old car. It was around thirty inches long and an inch and a half wide. One end was sharpened into a knifelike edge. To peel the logs, we used that sharpened edge. We had to punch the iron into the bark of the log and slowly pull it back, exposing the shiny white wood beneath. The sap from the log would splash onto my face, as the trees were so juicy in the beginning of the summer. Isä got more money at the paper mill in Cloquet for peeled logs, so it paid him to pay us.

Later in the summer the logs would have dried out so much that we couldn't peel them anymore. June is, of course, the height of the black fly and mosquito season, so we had to wear long-sleeved shirts and long-legged pants to protect ourselves. The temperature and humidity made this a sweaty job. Usually it was Marion and I who worked together as a team and we earned a nice little sum of money, maybe even as much as twenty dollars—a lot of money back then for a kid.

To entertain ourselves while we peeled logs, we told our own made-up stories. The stories were sometimes a continuation of soap operas that we would hear on the radio on rainy days when we didn't have to go into the woods. *Stella Dallas, My Gal Sal,* and *As the World Turns* were our format. In the 1930s and 1940s, soap operas filled the air and featured standard characters in real-life situations. The operas were sponsored by soap manufacturers, hence the name. We also had an ongoing series that we made up ourselves called "The Mystery of the Black-Haired Woman." We took turns making up the next episode.

By the end of June it was time to move on to other chores. The little wild strawberries were deliciously ripe by then, and we were paid ten cents a quart for picking them. My mother canned and froze them for our winter enjoyment. Then came the wild raspberries. We picked quarts and quarts of berries destined for canning, freezing, and jam. When there was nothing to pick, we were sent to the garden to pull weeds from the carrots, peas, beets, and all the other vegetables my mother had planted. Again, ten cents a row was the reward.

What did we do with all the money we earned? We bought our school clothes. (Smart thinking on my parents' part!) I wanted a pair of open-toed canvas pumps that I had lusted for all summer and had spotted in the window display at the Co-op store. They almost had a flavor they were so beautiful. Whenever I had a chance, I'd go into town with Isä and sneak over to the clothing department and smell these lovely red shoes. Mummy didn't think it was the best use of my dollars. I never realized until I became a parent the wisdom of my own parents.

Wild Berry Jam

8 cups washed, hulled strawberries or 12 cups washed blueberries
1½ cups sugar
Juice of 1 lemon

In a large saucepan, mix the berries with sugar and lemon juice. Set aside at room temperature for 3 hours. Then, simmer berries over medium-low heat, stirring occasionally with a wooden spoon and skimming foam as it rises, until the jam is thick and berries are soft (crush berries with the back of a spoon), about 15 minutes.

Sterilize four 1-pint mason jars by boiling jars, lids, and rims in a pot of boiling water for at least 20 minutes. Ladle the jam into the boiling hot jars and let stand at room temperature until the lids pop and are sealed.

Makes 4 delicious pints

Swimming

Northern Minnesota is known for its lakes and rivers. Ask anyone about them, and the Boundary Waters Canoe Area might be the first name that comes to mind. We never visited the BWCA. It was too far away and summertime was not a time for vacations. There was too much work to do. It wasn't possible for my parents to say, "We want to take a couple of weeks off for a canoe trip." What that meant is that we didn't take vacations, per se. Only when there was a big storm, lightning, thunder, and downpours did we have to (or as us kids would say, "got to") stay indoors and play games. Those were "vacation" days.

The St. Louis River ran by our farm. We were situated on a bend in the river that had a stretch of rapids where the water wasn't too deep and it was very cold. To get to the river we had to run down a path through the woods. This was a special treat in the heat of summer. What we called swimming was to find a rock on the bed of the river we could each call our own. If we could stay on that rock without being swept away, we were swimming. The rapids stretched for several hundred feet and the water was about three or four feet deep. A treacherous place, now that I think of it.

When we had a big summer storm, we looked forward to swimming—or what we called swimming—in the warmer water of the creek that fed the river.

It was always fun when we'd have a rainstorm and the water collected in the widened bends and turns of the "creek" that ran to the river from the woods next to our house and through the pasture behind the barn. The water was no more than two feet deep at its deepest point. The water would be muddy but it was warm. A day or so later, when it finally drained down to a trickle, it wasn't fun to "swim" in anymore.

On one warm summer day after a storm when the creek was swollen, Marion, Leonard, my two little sisters Betty Mae and Lillian, and I were swimming. Marion was showing off, singing her own mantra "sister knows how to swim so sister doesn't have to worry" as she dog-paddled across the widest point of the creek. It was a warm, muggy day, and in the sun-warmed water she stubbed her foot on a big rock and fell—*blub, blub*—into the water. At that point we got together and pulled her back to the muddy shore. Marion never lived down the bragging about her ability to swim.

From the time we were little kids, we associated the idea of swimming with just being in water outdoors—water heated by the sun. So, in my very early years—that was when only Leonard and I were ambulatory kids—swimming meant soaking in a round galvanized tub in sun-warmed water. We could splash all we wanted and we each had our own tub. That was swimming!

Cows in Wintertime

In the winter the cows were kept in the barn due to the immense amounts of snow that would fall. They had to have fresh water every day, and I was assigned the duty of pumping the water for the cows. The pump was little and the tank was very big, so I would climb onto a wooden platform and had to jump up and down with the pump handle. Sometimes the water never seemed to rise in the tank. At other times, when the pumping became routine, I'd daydream and the water would overflow. The water from the tank went through pipes to cups that were in front of the stanchioned cows, and while I pumped I would study the markings on the cows.

We made our own butter when I was very young. Later, we abandoned the practice in favor of selling whole milk that was separated in the creamery rather than on our farm.

Nätti (the name is Finnish for "cute") was my family's favorite cow. She was reddish brown with bright white spots on her that seemed to outline images. Sometimes her spots looked like profiles of people, sometimes like animals. Nättie's eyes seemed to bulge on her thin head. She was the oldest cow in the barn and her horns were curly. Isä used to say, "You could count her years by the rings on her horns."

Lizzie was a honey-blond cow. She was always fat and had a big udder. I used to think that Lizzie would make a perfect grandmother if she were a person. Lizzie was slow and peaceful and next oldest to Nättie.

Pansy was *my* cow. I had such a personal attachment to her. She was pretty, bright black and white, and streamlined—I always thought that if Pansy were a person she would be a pretty aunt with a good figure. I remember holding her tail while Mummy or Isä milked her. I was proud to hold Pansy's curly tail because she was my cow!

Tillie was black and white, too, and awfully temperamental. She kicked for no reason at all sometimes. Her manure was always soft and would really splash. I thought she did that on purpose. Tillie gave lots of milk but always had bull calves.

Lola was big boned, didn't give much milk, and I milked her. She was a light-blond cow, and the athletic type, I thought. I remember the time she

Beloved Pansy, my favorite cow.

placed her hoof mark on the chest of my pretty pink sunsuit. The stain never really washed out.

Then there was one we called "Crazy Cow." She jumped, kicked, and swatted her tail for no reason. She was small but gave a lot of milk. All her daughters turned out to be crazy cows, too.

Three Titter was a cow who had one damaged teat and could only be milked from three of her teats. Her milk production matched that of the average cows in the barn, so we kept her.

The Floodwood Creamery kept a record of the names of all the cows in our barn. When heifers gave birth and began producing milk, they needed to have a name. Isä was "out of names" and when our cow Lulu's heifer became a milk producer and had to be named, he named her "Ulul"—spelling the name of her mother backward.

One day Nätti went missing. She was old but still gave lots of milk, and she had just freshened that spring (which means she had had a calf). Cows in the springtime were let out to pasture when the new grass became juicy and green. By evening and morning of each day, their udders were nearly bursting with milk.

It was a sunny morning when I was around twelve years old that Nätti went missing. We searched the woods and brush behind the east field where the cows had been grazing. We even searched the riverbank, where the cows seldom went. We called the neighbors and they joined in the search. No luck.

What seemed strange was that we couldn't hear her bell either. Nätti was the leader of the herd—an office appointed by her peers. She was always at the head of the line as we called the cows in for milking at morning and evening. My father had a special call for the cows: "Sipu, sipu, sipu." Those words don't actually mean anything, but if anyone used those words, the cows would come ambling straight to the barn.

"Sipu, sipu, sipu!" we would call, and there would come old Nättie at the head of the line, her bell swinging from left to right, followed by the remaining twenty-nine members of the mostly Guernsey herd. This morning the beckoning call failed to bring in the leader. Two days went by and still no trace of our favorite lead cow.

There was no evidence, either, of Nättie being stolen by cattle rustlers. No, she was much too old to be worth that kind of effort; besides, we lived at the dead end of a county road and the pastures were hidden behind groves of poplar, aspen, and pine trees. It would have been impossible for anybody to come in with a truck because our driveway was a full quarter mile long and they would be in full view of the house and the barn.

Nättie had obviously lost her way in the woods. After all, she was an old cow. Do cows get Alzheimer's disease?

Tillie, Lola, Lulu, Ulul, Daisy, Violet, and all the rest plodded into the yard behind the barn, likely out of habit and looking forward to relief because their udders were uncomfortable and bulging with milk. If only they could talk. The faithful herd filed into the barn and headed right for their own stalls. Stanchions closed, we washed their udders, attached the cups of the milking machines, and relieved each one of her burden. After the machines were removed, we "stripped" each cow of the remaining milk in their udders (if we didn't do that, they would gradually produce less milk as time went on—kind of like rechargeable batteries that have not fully depleted their energy before being recharged). Each cow would be turned out, one at a time, through the back door of the barn when they were finished. Each would head to the watering tank for a nice long drink and then amble out to the pasture again.

That particular day when Nättie was missing, there was a pall over the farm. My father, Mummy, the neighbors, hired men, and various relatives combed the woods listening for any sound of life as they searched for the missing cow. The search continued for three days.

Early in the morning of the fourth day, Isä (who I always thought had a clairvoyant sense about him) had a dream in which he was told to head east of the usual pasture that ran toward a swampy area surrounded by alder brush. Convinced of his vision, he headed toward that spot as soon as daylight broke. Sure enough, he heard a muffled groan.

There, sunk into the muck, was our beloved Nättie! Only the ridge of her back was above the mud, her head was pointed upward, and she was still breathing.

I don't know how they did it, but with a tractor, ropes, pulleys, and straps, my father, mother, relatives, and hired men managed to pull old Nätti out of the quicksand. Another few hours and she would have been buried alive. She had been rescued just in time.

Nättie was laid on a sledge and brought back to the barn, where we scrubbed her down with warm water. She drank gallons of water. Her once plump body was bony and her udders were thin. Isä was advised to "put her down," but he just couldn't. Nättie lived several more years, but never really regained her milk production. That was okay. We loved her until she died.

A few years later, as a sophomore or junior in high school, I took a class that combined public speaking and English. At school, I was always a little afraid of baring my soul and talking about my life on our farm. All through school, even my friends wouldn't come out to the farm. Ever. I was a country kid. But I really wanted to talk to others about my life on the farm and the things I loved there. For instance, I wanted to explain my love for the cows in the barn. I loved them so much. So one day, for my public speaking class, I wrote a speech about that.

When it came time to read our writing aloud, I honestly wasn't trying to be funny. I was seriously describing the pleasures of milking a cow on a forty-degrees-below-zero morning. When it is that cold, I can't think of a cozier place to be than the barn. The sounds of the cows munching on the hay in the manger in front of them, with the strains of Famous Lashua the Singing Cowboy in the air. Mummy always said that cows were happier when there was music in the air. It made the cows "drop their milk" more easily when the barn is full of the strains of a song. We always had a radio on, and sometimes I would sing along with the tune.

I loved to be perched on a short, three-legged stool, my head against the warm belly of a cow as I squirted milk beginning with the *zing, zing* into an empty pail that soon grew to a *swoosh, swoosh* as the milk grew deeper and the foam built on top of the white liquid. The cows were my warm friends, especially on a bitterly cold morning. I had learned by then that each cow radiates about 4,300 BTUs per hour! Now that's why a barn is a cozy place to be.

So all I could think of writing and talking about at the moment was how pleasant it was to be milking cows on a forty-below day. I proceeded to tell twenty of my classmates all about it. As I told the story, the teacher, Miss Wennerstrom—who was about as wide as she was tall—began to laugh so hard she had to sit down. She began to jiggle all over and then laugh out loud.

This made the whole class laugh before I could even finish the story. As I read she laughed harder, and then the whole class started laughing. I wondered if the class could smell barn on me. Seriously, though, I just wanted to let my teacher and my classmates know where I was coming from. My story didn't make any peer points for me, but I did get a good grade in the class—Miss Wennerstrom rarely smiled. I couldn't see what was so funny.

Finnish Baked Cheese (Leipäjuusto)

The formula for this recipe is based on one that Lauri Sauko (director of Salolampi language camp) shared. It enhances the milk with extra milk powder and heavy cream. The dry milk adds a great deal of bulk to the cheese. Rennet can be ordered through the Internet from cheesemaking supply houses.

1 gallon skim milk
3 cups instant dry milk (Lauri says Carnation works best)
1 quart heavy cream
1 rennet tablet
¼ cup water
1 teaspoon salt

Mix milk, dry milk, and cream well in a large, heavy pot and place over lowest heat until milk reaches 110°F.

Crush rennet into the water and add to the milk; stir in the salt. Cover and do not stir anymore. Turn off the heat and let stand 1 hour until milk curdles and looks like a custard. It is okay to let it stand 2 to 3 hours (in fact, some recipes call for putting the pot in the refrigerator at this point to stand overnight).

With a long spatula or knife, cut the curd into 1-inch squares. The curd and whey should separate. If curd is very soft, place over low heat again for about half an hour.

Line a colander with dampened cheesecloth. Place over a large bowl or pan to collect the whey. Pour milk mixture into the cloth-lined colander. Drain well.

Transfer curds to a large rimmed cookie sheet or pizza pan. Press into a firm, evenly thick round cake.

Broil until cheese shrinks from sides of the pan. Pour off whey. Invert cheese onto another pan and broil to golden brown. (I had to invert mine several times onto another pan and broil again.)

This recipe makes a large squeaky cheese, which can be cut into portions, wrapped, and refrigerated until you're ready to eat it.

Venison

The fat and happy deer grazed on oats in the forty-acre field planted to the west of our farmhouse. When Mummy would discreetly tell Isä that we were out of meat, his response was that he would "tend to that tonight."

Isä would strap on his headlight that night and go out on our acreage and shoot a deer. We preferred the young deer instead of the old bucks, which were tough and had a strong wild flavor.

With one crack of the gun the deer was felled, dragged to the shed, hung, and stripped of its innards. The liver was a huge treat. We sliced it thin, fried it in butter, and enjoyed it for breakfast the next day.

Isä's take on this? "I feed 'em, I eat 'em." In fact, we wasted nothing. Even the hide was taken to a place where it was tanned and usually made into the buckskin mitts we wore in the winter.

We had a heavy butcher knife with a rounded blade in the kitchen when I was growing up. Isä kept it sharp on his sharpening stone, which consisted of a circular whetstone about the size of a bicycle wheel, on an axle-like frame. He would sit on a wooden plank and turn the stone, which would go through water that was held in half of a rubber tire and was mounted beneath the wheel. He made the wheel turn by pedaling, and water would splash to the sides as the knife gained its razor-sharp edge. He sharpened not just the butcher knives that way but also the triangular cutting blades of the hay mower and anything else that required a sharp edge.

With that sharpened knife, he cut the raw venison into roasts or chunks. The roasts were wrapped and brined or canned. Before we had electricity and a deep-freezer, we brined the larger pieces of meat. Mummy also packed smaller chunks of meat into wide-mouth quart-sized canning jars and added a teaspoon or so of salt. Because they had not yet purchased a big pressure cooker for canning, she put the jars in the oven of the woodstove and then fired it up until the oven was hot enough to cook and can the meat. The canned venison was deliciously soft and tender and became the basis for all kinds of our favorite dishes, from soups to sandwiches to casseroles. Sometimes we just ate it right out of the jar.

One time, after one of the butcherings and when we were all out doing barn chores, we heard a huge explosion in the house. The venison-filled jars in the wood-fired oven had exploded and there was meat hanging everywhere in the kitchen along with glass shards. When one jar had exploded, so did the rest of them, causing a chain reaction. Laughing and crying at once, Mummy cleaned up the mess. Shortly after that they bought a big pressure cooker.

The Best Venison Liver and Onions

This was a delicacy we had the morning after a young deer was butchered. The liver was cut into very thin slices and we enjoyed it for breakfast.

About 2 pounds sliced young venison liver
¼ cup butter, divided
2 large Vidalia onions, sliced into rings
2 cups all-purpose flour, or as needed
Salt and pepper to taste

Gently rinse liver slices under cold water, and place in a medium bowl. Pour in enough milk to cover. Let stand while preparing onions. (If the venison is from an older animal, you'll need to soak it in milk for a couple of hours to reduce the bitter taste.)

Melt 2 tablespoons of butter in a large skillet over medium heat. Separate onion rings, and sauté them in butter until soft. Remove onions and melt remaining butter in the skillet. Season the flour with salt and pepper, and put it in a shallow dish or on a plate. Drain milk from liver, and coat slices in the flour mixture.

When the butter has melted, turn the heat up to medium-high, and place the coated liver slices in the pan. Cook until nice and brown on the bottom. Turn, and cook on the other side until browned. Add onions, and reduce heat to medium. Cook a bit longer to taste. Our family prefers the liver to just barely retain a pinkness on the inside when you cut to check. Enjoy!

Visits from Aunts and Uncles

I close my eyes and visualize myself during a favorite, peaceful evening in my childhood. I am tucked into bed. It is a davenport that unfolds to make a bed. It is big and heavy, with wood on the topside of the arms. It smelled like wet leather in the summertime. The bed is cozy and comfortable.

I was about four years old and there were three of us children at the time—Leonard, Marion, and me. There were three rooms in our farmhouse at the time, the living room, where Marion and I would sleep; a bedroom, where Mummy and Isä slept; and a narrow bed for my little brother, who had been born deaf. When Auntie Esther visited, she slept with Marion and me because we had the largest bed. We didn't mind at all. The kitchen was big, and behind the woodstove there was a tall, black "slop pail." That's where us kids would go pee in the wintertime because Mummy thought it was too cold for us to run along the snowy path to the outhouse.

The outhouse had two holes, one that was bigger and higher and one for us kids that was smaller, on a lower shelf. Each hole had a wooden lid with a handle. We didn't have toilet paper, so we wiped ourselves using pages torn from the previous year's Montgomery Ward catalog. I really preferred to use pieces torn from the newspaper, but newspapers had only a few pages so the supply didn't last long. When there was nothing left of the catalog but the shiny pages, you had to crinkle them up so the paper wouldn't be too slippery to do the job.

In 1940, when I was six years old, the Rural Electric Association extended service to our area and our farm was wired for electricity. That was about the time that Isä decided to expand the house, and with the help of the hired men and our uncles, he added another bedroom and a bathroom with a "flush" toilet—which meant that the house was plumbed, with a water tank and a sewage system. A stairway from our living room was added so that we could have a bedroom in the attic. It wasn't heated.

I remember one night, prior to the renovation, when my favorite aunt was visiting for the night. She was my father's sister—pretty, slim, with dark wavy hair and with the same name as my mother. I called her "Auntie Esther."

One night I could hear the two Esthers laughing and giggling all night. They laughed and they giggled and they giggled and they laughed. Then I heard Mummy say, "Here, pee in my shoe." Auntie Esther laughed even harder. I pretended I was fast asleep. I wondered what they were laughing about. Later, I found out they had cornered a mouse.

Aunt Ida was the mail-order bride of Isä's brother Edward. I could never have imagined Edward courting any woman, and besides, the "pickings" in northern Minnesota at the time were not great, so it made perfect sense that he would fill out a form and order a wife. Uncle Edward specified that she had to be Finnish, Lutheran, and a good cook and housekeeper. Ida filled the bill perfectly.

The thing about Ida was that she was rather "fancy," having spent some years in New York as a cook for influential people—such as the Henry Morgenthau household (when he was secretary of the treasury) and other luminaries. She actually would come to live in Floodwood only when her employers were out of the country on vacation, usually three months or so at a time.

When Edward and Ida became engaged, Ida thought that Ed couldn't afford a decent engagement ring, so she bought one herself in New York. She inspected my mother's engagement ring and proclaimed it "Seep!" (Cheap). Mummy's answer to this insult was, "But Ted bought it for me with his own money!"

Whenever Ida came home, she and Ed would make the rounds visiting all the relatives. She was full of stories. Like when we talked about how we got samples of new products in the mail. She got the sample products in little bottles that the company representative hung on the doorknob of her New York apartment. Ida was angry that people would steal her samples, such as the time someone took her sample of Listerine mouthwash. "So," she said, "I fix them! I piss in a bottle and hung it on the doorknob. Heh, heh, they stole it!"

Ida was less than five feet tall, with beady eyes and a head of curly strawberry blond hair. She always carried a fat purse, wore Cuban-heeled black shoes, and talked incessantly about her sister's girl, Barbara, whom she referred to as "Barba" rolling the *r*'s. She would say, "Barba has tin leks!" (Barbara has thin legs) when she looked at my muscular legs.

Today I credit my aunt Ida for my white hair. My hair began to turn white (I hesitate to say gray!) when I was in my thirties. So, I colored my hair, but didn't do it regularly enough, and one day when Ida and Ed were visiting, she cocked her head just like a bird and studied my hair and asked, "How come dat Peetsis hair is dat kine two tone?"

I vowed at that moment to go natural!

Aunt Ellen was a chain-smoker and would light her next cigarette from the one she was just finishing. She was the wife of my uncle Jack, who was an older brother of Isä—and Ellen was probably the reason for Edward's decision to order a bride from New York. Ellen was a local who seemed to know all the men around. It was said that Jack was impotent, even though they had three children. There was Edwin, who was three when Jack and Ellen were married. Then there was Raymond, who bore no resemblance to the family. Mummy reported that when Ellen was pregnant, she had said in Finnish, "Well, I don't know if the baby is Jack's, but I know for sure it is mine!"

Ellen kept an immaculate house (except for the stench of cigarette smoke). She was very particular about how the "dishies" were washed, dried, and placed in the cupboard. Her electric stove was always scrubbed and looked like new. The oven sparkled. You couldn't find a speck of dust on any of her furniture, and she carefully washed the sheets on every bed once a week. But you couldn't breathe the air!

Uncle Jack was the one that we referred to as our "one-armed uncle." I remember him when he had two arms. One day when he was on Highway 53, his car ran out of gas and he walked back to a gas station with a gas can. When he was walking back to his car with his left arm stuck out to balance the weight of the full can, a speeding car swiped him, taking off his left arm just below the elbow. They never found his hand and wrist, nor did they catch the driver. Ellen especially regretted that his wedding ring and watch were gone. Jack was fitted with a prosthetic wooden arm from the elbow down, and a pair of hooks instead of a hand. Jack continued to earn his living as a carpenter. He was lucky, he said, that he was right handed, and he could hold the nails with his left hand/hook and never hurt himself if his missed the nail with the hammer.

I was about five years old when I can remember the man who later became "Uncle John" visiting our home. He was courting my aunt Esther, who was staying with us for a while to help my mother after the birth of my little sister.

Uncle John lived in Brookston, a village about ten miles away, and I thought he was so handsome. He had a twinkle in his eye and seemed always to be smiling and always had a tall tale to tell. He would usually give me two or three shiny copper pennies. My aunt Esther taught me how to stack the pennies in the middle of a hanky and tie a knot just above them. When I went into town with Isä, I bought penny candy such as wax lips, candy buttons, Necco wafers, and root beer barrels. I usually chose those that were five for a penny so that I had enough to share with my brother and sisters at home. One Saturday evening Uncle John made me a wonderful promise. He promised to take me with him on his "milk route." He was employed by the Floodwood Creamery to drive the milk truck around the countryside to pick up milk from farmers in the area. His route went northwest along Highway 2, through the towns of Wawina, Swan River, and and then south to Jacobson. Oh, I was so excited! I kept asking him about the towns I would see. He told me that Jacobson was such a big city that you had to really watch it when you crossed the street because there were so many streetcars and people.

"There are really tall buildings in Jacobson," he told me. "It is really hard to find your way around in such a big city."

"Should I wear my prettiest dress for the day?" I wondered out loud.

"Oh, yes!" he told me. "People in Jacobson are dressed really fancy!"

I could hardly wait. I chose my princess dress that had sections in various shades of blue. I had a pin that looked like a real pair of miniature sunglasses—about the size that would fit on a mouse. I put that pin just below my left shoulder, far enough down so that I could look at it once in a while. I put on pale-blue anklets and wore my strappy white sandals. I was sure I was dressed for the occasion.

Uncle John's milk route started early in the morning—when it was still a little chilly outside, but the cab of his truck was cozy. We bumped along Highway 2, the truck grinding along as he shifted gears. Then he would turn the truck into a farmyard and back the truck up to the milk house, go into the milk house, and hoist the ten-gallon cans of milk into the back of the truck. Uncle John would climb back into the cab, start up the truck, and we'd bump along to the next farmyard. I sat eagerly on the edge of my seat watching carefully for that huge city to come into view.

I kept asking him about Jacobson, that big and special town that I had never heard of before. I was so excited to see this big city with all the street-cars and fancily trimmed windows. The story grew taller.

"Many famous people live in Jacobson," Uncle John told me.

"Who?" I asked, becoming more fascinated and curious as the time went on.

"Oh, there are the Siermalas and the Ruzynskys and the Minkkinens!"

I was truly impressed and getting more eager all the time to see this wonderful metropolis.

"When will we get to Jacobson?" I'd ask anxiously.

"Oh, about eleven thirty." We chugged along turning into one farm after another. I'd feel the bump of the milk cans as they were hoisted into the back of the truck. I'd hear the slam of the doors and the crunch of Uncle John's footsteps as he came back to the cab to start the truck again, and off we went to yet another driveway. It seemed to take forever.

"Are we there yet?"

"Almost," he replied. "Jacobson is just around the corner."

Then, suddenly, he stopped the truck in front of a building with a sign in front that read "Jacobson, Minnesota Post Office." Uncle John said, "Well, here we are!" We were in Jacobson.

I started to laugh. Uncle John had been pulling my leg and I was gullible enough not to see through all of his tall tales—that had only grown taller—about Jacobson. He did buy me a double ice-cream cone as a reward for being patient.

The story about Jacobson remained our favorite reminiscence for the rest of his life. Uncle John fought cancer for seven years and endeared himself to the staff at St. Luke's Hospital in Duluth. He died on Easter Sunday morning in 1966.

When Uncle John died, our son, Greg, was six years old. Greg had been curious about what happens after we die and we talked about it a lot. On the way home after the funeral, Greg's comment was, "Now Uncle John knows the big secret!"

Orange Date-Nut Cake

Drop-in company was a common occurrence in the summertime. Plus, summertime was when we seemed to have a lot of family traffic, hired men, and neighbors around. We felt we could never be caught without some kind of *kahvileipä*, that is, something to go with coffee.

This is the perfect cake for any occasion and it keeps well—that is, if it isn't all eaten up right away! It's moist and delicious because it's doused with orange juice syrup just after it is removed from the oven. We usually baked this cake in a 9- by 13-inch rectangular pan, but once in a while, we'd bake it in a fluted tube pan or a Bundt pan.

1½ cups sugar, divided
¾ cup (1½ sticks) butter, at room temperature
2 large eggs
2 teaspoons freshly grated orange zest
2½ cups all-purpose flour
1 teaspoon baking powder

1 teaspoon baking soda
1 cup chopped pitted dates
1 cup chopped walnuts
1 cup buttermilk
1 cup fresh orange juice

Preheat the oven to 350°F. Butter a 9- by 13-inch baking pan or a 10-inch fluted tube pan.

In a large mixing bowl, cream ¾ cup of the sugar and the butter together until smooth. Add the eggs and beat until light. Stir in the orange zest. In another bowl, mix together the flour, baking powder, and baking soda. Put the dates and walnuts into yet another small bowl and mix with 1 tablespoon of the flour mixture. Add the flour mixture and buttermilk alternately to the creamed mixture and beat until the batter is light. Fold in the dates and nuts. Turn the batter into the prepared pan.

Bake for 35 to 40 minutes for the 9- by 13-inch cake, or 55 to 60 minutes for the tube pan, or until a wooden skewer comes out clean. (We used to take a piece of straw from a corn broom to use as a tester.)

Meanwhile, combine the orange juice and remaining sugar in a small saucepan. Heat to simmering and pour over the hot cake as soon as you take it out of the oven.

Cool the cake in the pan on a wire rack. Invert the tube cake onto a serving plate or cut squares from the 9- by 13-inch cake.

Makes about 16 servings

My Twelfth Birthday

We were a big family. So when it came to holidays and birthdays, there was no need to invite more people to have a party. At least that's what my mother always said. She would pretend that she didn't remember it was a birthday. She would secretly bake a cake, behave in a nonchalant way toward the birthday son or daughter, and present the cake as a surprise.

For some reason I especially remember my twelfth birthday. My birthday is in July, always just in the middle of haymaking season. As usual, it was hot and humid, and I worked harder than ever in the hayfield on my birthday. I started the day sitting on the metal seat of the hay mower bumping over the fields, pulled by "the joker" my dad was driving. The long blade of the hay mower whirred down the tall grass.

The joker was a kind of tractor that my dad had made from a four-cylinder Model A, so it had a driver's seat and steering wheel—everything else was exposed. It was just strong enough to pull a mower, a hay rake, or a hay wagon and used less gas than the big tractor.

My job was to lift the cutting blade so that it would miss rocks or bumps that could possibly cause damage to the blades. We circled the forty acres dozens of times, cutting a five-foot swath at a time that created a kind of continuous spiral until finally, every last blade was down. I loved the sweet smell of freshly cut hay—especially when it was alfalfa or clover.

We stopped for a break in midmorning. Mummy brought fresh cookies and a canning jar of nectar for me and a thermos of hot coffee mixed with sugar and milk for my dad. We sat in the shade of the joker as we enjoyed our refreshments.

I was absolutely certain that she had forgotten all about my birthday.

After the break, I mounted the seat on the hay rake that Isä had unhitched from the mower and attached to the joker. Off we rode to the far field to rake the dried hay that we had cut the day before. This was a bigger job for me because I had to pull the lever to dump the hay into long rows that later we'd rake into piles by hand. Then we would pitch the hay onto the hay wagon and haul it all to the barn to be stored in the hayloft.

It was hot and humid, and the hay felt prickly on my skin. My job now was to set the slings on the wagon and tramp down the hay as Isä and Mummy pitched forkfuls onto the platform. When the hay wagon was loaded I got to ride on top as we slowly drove to the barn.

At the barn we attached the ends of the slings to a hook at the end of the rope that was hanging down from the rounded top of the thirty-five-foot-high barn. It was a complicated system of tracks, ropes, and pulleys that we used to lift a whole load of hay all at once into the hayloft.

When everything was set, Isä connected the tractor to the other end of the rope on the opposite side of the barn. Slowly the load of bundled hay rose up onto the track and finally sailed into the loft. I had to give a really strong tug on the lead rope to trip the locks, drop the hay, and then pull the slings back to the ground so that we could go out for another load.

Dinner (which I now call lunch) had been hurried that day. A series of thunderstorms had been predicted, and the hay had to be in the barn before they hit. Usually, Mummy and Isä would "rest" right after the noon meal in the side bedroom, the door locked tight with a butter knife stuck into the frame of the door. That day was different, however, and we went right back into the hayfield after eating. There was no sign of a birthday cake.

By late afternoon all the hay was finally in the loft, the air grew hotter and heavier, and we were ready for a break. Exhausted and feeling itchy from scratchy dry hay (that had dried thistles in it as well), we headed toward the house.

There, in front of the house, was a big, plaid blanket spread out on the lawn with wrapped gifts, a pitcher of nectar, and a stack of plates. Then Mummy came out with the birthday cake lit with twelve candles. Leonard, Marion, Lillian, Betty Mae, Eugene, and Rudy all yelled "Surprise!"

The orange chiffon cake tasted unusually delicious. The strawberry nectar tasted great, especially because I was so thirsty. But what felt the best of all was that Mummy hadn't forgotten my birthday. I felt warm and loved.

Isä took a picture of me with the Brownie camera after I opened all my gifts: I got a pair of bloomers from Mummy and Isä, a little vial of Blue Waltz Perfume from Marion, a straw hat from Lillian and Betty Mae, and a dog collar from Leonard that I could put on his dog. Eugene and Rudy were only four and three that year, but they, too, wanted to give me something. I got a weasel tail from Eugene and a dead frog from Rudy. Nancy, who was just four months old, was lying on a baby blanket.

It was a wonderful birthday.

No Recipe Needed

There were always cinnamon rolls in our farm kitchen for snacks or to go with coffee. Mummy felt that the yeast-raised, slightly sweet rolls were much healthier than sugar- and fat-loaded cookies. She baked a huge batch of coffee-glazed cinnamon rolls at least once or sometimes two or three times a week, depending on what was going on. If we had many hired hands around, as in the spring for planting, or in the fall when Isä had lots of outdoor work to get done, that's when we needed more kahvileipä.

When I searched her files for the recipe, I found only recipes from family and friends, but not Mummy's cinnamon rolls. Reflecting on this, I remember her saying—"I just make them." She didn't need a recipe.

Here's how it went. She would take the big tin bread pan down and smash a cake of yeast with a little sugar until the yeast made a smooth, soft paste. To that she would add three or four quarts of lukewarm milk and a little more sugar. Then she'd add the salt, some fresh eggs, sometimes six, sometimes eight (eggs make the dough nice and tender). Next, she'd start adding flour, slowly at first so that she could beat the batter until it was nice and smooth. She'd taste the batter and add enough sugar to make it taste good. Not too much. Then more flour, keeping the dough smooth. Before kneading the dough, she thought it was a good idea to let it "rest" for fifteen minutes or even half an hour until the yeast had a chance to permeate the batter and it became puffy. Then she would sprinkle more flour over the top and begin turning the dough over on itself (she did this by hand in her big bread pan). As she turned the dough over on itself, she would sprinkle more flour over and punch it into the center of the mixture. When the dough had enough flour added, it would no longer stick to her fingers. Then, she'd check to see there was no more "loose" flour and turn the dough over so the top of the batch was smooth. She would cover the dough with a muslin towel and then put on the pan's metal cover and put it into a warm place to rise. This would take an hour or so.

Once the bulging pan of dough had risen, she'd cut off about an eighth of it and slap it down onto a lightly floured countertop and roll it out to about ½-inch thickness. Next, she'd spread the dough with soft butter and sprinkle it generously with cinnamon sugar and roll it up. With a knife (or sometimes with a string) she would cut the roll into 1-inch slices and place them on a greased cookie sheet. This she repeated until all eight portions of the dough were shaped into rolls. There were about a dozen cookie sheets of dish-towel-covered rising rolls on every surface in the kitchen. On the woodstove there would be a syrup of coffee and sugar (about ¼ cup sugar to each cup of coffee), boiling. The rolls were baked about 10 minutes or so in a 375°F wood-fired oven. Then, when she took the pale-golden rolls out, Mummy would slather them with the coffee syrup to make them juicy. The sixteen dozen rolls that her recipe made sometimes lasted two days!

Here's a smaller rendition of the juicy cinnamon rolls adapted to my favorite "refrigerator dough method":

Mummy's "Juicy" Cinnamon Rolls

2 packages active dry yeast	½ cup nonfat dry milk
1 cup warm water	2 eggs
½ cup melted butter	1 teaspoon salt
½ cup sugar	About 4 cups all-purpose flour

Filling

½ cup soft butter	1 tablespoon cinnamon
½ cup brown sugar	

Coffee glaze

1 cup powdered sugar	hot strong coffee

In a large bowl, combine the yeast and warm water. Stir. Let stand about 5 minutes or until the yeast foams. Stir in the butter, sugar, dry milk, eggs, and salt. Beat in flour, 1 cup at a time, until the dough is too stiff to mix; you may reach that stage before you have added all the flour. Cover and refrigerate 2 hours or up to 4 days.

On a lightly floured board, cut the dough into two parts. Roll one part at a time to make a rectangle 12 inches square. Spread with ¼ cup soft butter. Mix the sugar and cinnamon and sprinkle with half the brown sugar mixture over the dough. Roll up into a firm, log-shaped roll. Cut diagonally to make about 1-inch slices. Place rolls on a greased baking sheet and let rise for 30 minutes or until golden.

Preheat the oven to 350°F. Bake the rolls for 10 to 15 minutes or until golden. Mix the powdered sugar with enough hot coffee to make a thin glaze. Brush baked rolls with the glaze.

Makes 24 large cinnamon rolls

Feed Sack Fashion

There was a time in the 1940s when we were able to get free fabric by using colorfully printed feed sacks, which we would purchase at the Co-op in Floodwood. Isä had a good eye for selecting the nicest prints and was wise enough to buy more than one sack in the same print. It usually took two to three sacks to sew a simple dress. The feed sacks were used instead of many barrels for the storage and transport of flour and animal feed, which we purchased regularly for the cows. Animal feed sacks were larger than the hundred-pound flour sacks, so they were much easier to work with.

When I was in 4-H, I had to keep a record of everything I did for the projects I had signed up for. In my 4-H clothing record I described the dresses, blouses, and shirts that I sewed for myself and for my brothers and sisters out of feed sacks. Also, I enjoyed making Christmas gifts of clothing for the family. In my record I describe a baby dress I made for a shower out of a printed feed sack.

My report as I wrote it: "I like my clothing project because I just love to sew. My ambition to sew has really been valuable to the whole family. Whenever anyone needs a blouse, shirt, skirt or dress, I just sew it. Since there are so many in the family there is always sewing to do.

"Every time I finish a garment I make a report on it on a sheet of paper. By the end of the year I was really surprised to find how they had added up and how much I saved by sewing.

"This past year I have learned a lot about working with corduroy and this year the sister dresses are made from it."

Up until this point I had been sewing on a treadle sewing machine and each year made identical "sister dresses" for my four sisters and myself. For Christmas in 1949, Isä bought Mummy a new electric Singer sewing machine. The sewing machine came with a booklet that had a series of sewing lessons, which I gladly took.

Again, from my 4-H clothing record at the time: "I planned to make a lot of dresses for myself, but the majority of the sewing I ended up doing was for others in the family. I don't mind though, as it would be selfish of me to sew mostly for myself. The money I saved by sewing will almost pay for the cost of the sewing machine. When making a garment I seldom used a pattern because I liked to create my own designs. The Duluth *Herald* and *News-Tribune* had a lot of cute patterns for sale, and I clipped them from the paper and pinned them in a string on the wall of my bedroom for inspiration."

I used the pictures of the patterns as ideas for making my own. The patterns were, we thought, too expensive when it is so easy to make them myself.

The sister dresses I made were different every year. One year *Seventeen* magazine came to Floodwood to do a story on teenagers at our school, and they published a photo of my four sisters and me next to a haystack on the farm. The dresses were identical—pale-green voile, with a square inset—my own design, as I didn't have the money nor could I find the patterns in all five sizes.

This photograph was published in *Seventeen* magazine in an article on teenagers in small towns. I made the clothes that my siblings and I are wearing.

Later, when I took home economics at the university, my grades in sewing were not good. We always said that the clothing construction professor would take off points for a "wiggle in a stitch." Sewing garments had been, in my experience, something done out of necessity—not in search of perfection. Even though I had done a lot of sewing for the family and myself, I did not get good grades on the garments that I entered into the St. Louis County Fair. My penchant for speed and efficiency showed. I didn't press seams properly or finish hems in a beautiful way. That cost me points on the professional scale.

Hired Men

Anyone who has lived on a farm in northern Minnesota knows that farming isn't the most lucrative endeavor, regardless of how beautiful the countryside might be. My dad was resourceful, though, and coupled the farming life with that of a lumberjack—not uncommon among Finns at that time. He would lease acres of woods from St. Louis County and then harvest the lumber from that acreage. He hired men to help him out.

When the workload was heavy, extra "hands" were necessary. Isä would hire a couple of guys from "Boy's Town"—a strip of shacks along the edge of Floodwood, where old bachelors lived when they weren't helping out on a farm, usually on weekends after blowing their earnings at the local bar.

Although addicted to alcohol and nicotine, these old Finnish guys had a gentle nature to them. As kids, we even loved their names. There was Hippa Heikki, Haapa Koski, and "Pissa Antti." Henry Martimo and Pete Martimo were brothers who worked on the farm. The men all told us funny stories about animals in the woods, dogs, birds. Simple stories, really. Mummy didn't like them because they were drunks. Isä thought they were great because they were "good workers." They'd work all week, expect to get paid on Friday, then would blow it all on booze over the weekend. Monday morning they'd stagger back to work, pants wet on the inside of their legs.

To keep them happy, Isä sometimes had a little extra elixir on hand, which he had the habit of dipping into as well. This didn't make Mummy happy.

Just because these guys were drunks, it didn't mean that we didn't like them. Pete Martimo, for instance, was a really fun guy. When he laughed, he started out with a "heh, heh" that developed into a full-fledged roar. As he laughed, his skinny body vibrated in waves, like the branches on poplar trees. Pete later decided to dry up and quit drinking cold turkey. Mummy respected Pete a lot for that. But Pete's brother, Henry, continued on with the booze. He was taller, more muscular, and could physically handle much bigger trees. Then there was Andrew Leppi. We called him "Pissa Antti" because he was incontinent, especially when he drank.

One time when all the hired men were sitting around the breakfast table eating bowls full of Malt-O-Meal, Henry Martimo sneezed with his mouth

Henry and Pete Martimo at the shack they built in the woods about a mile from our farmhouse. The road that leads to this spot is now called Martima Road (misspelled by whoever names county roads!).

full and sprayed cereal all over me. I looked like a sandblasted ceiling and had to wash my face, hair, and all my clothes before I felt comfortable again.

Some of the bachelors in Boy's Town were too old for heavy lumberjack work. Isä would hire those men to pick potatoes in September. There was Hippa Heikki and Haapa Koski, and we kids would march around repeating their names because they were so rhythmic. Both Hippa Heikki and Haapa Koski were bent little old men who wore overalls and plaid flannel shirts. Isä would give them a ride back into Boy's Town at the end of the day.

We housed a couple of other men in what we called the "carpenter shack," a little building on the farm that held cots, a couple of benches, and a few pegs for hanging their jackets, caps, and overalls at night. These old men slept in their long johns, which Mummy would wash once a week. These guys were homeless men who didn't live in Boy's Town. The shack wasn't very big and I have wondered how they kept themselves entertained, as we never saw them playing games or reading. They would relax outside under the trees when the weather was nice, smoking cigarettes and telling stories until it was dark. Then, I suppose, they just fell into bed, exhausted from their day's work.

Paul Long's Wife's Rieska

Paul Long was a man Isä hired from time to time when he needed extra hands. It was a hot and humid July day in the middle of haymaking when Paul Long and his wife dropped in for a visit. The temperature and humidity hovered at about a hundred. Mummy set the coffee table with sliced cheese, butter, and salami with cookies along with slices of Zinsmaster bread. It was a rare thing for us to have "bought bread," which was a treat for us kids—we loved the "bread that folds" because we had it about once a year.

Mrs. Long was mortified. The following week she came over with a loaf of rieska and exclaimed (in Finnish), "This is homemade bread made with Occident flour!" She thought we had "bought bread" all the time—and said it was terrible for such a large family to be deprived of healthy homemade bread.

Mummy felt really insulted. She wasn't able even to eat Mrs. Long's bread, she felt so bad.

Here's a recipe very similar to Mrs. Long's bread. It is a simple bread that is baked free-form on a cookie sheet and turns out to be not much more than an inch and a half thick. Even though rieska is typically a quick bread, this one includes yeast for leavening.

Mrs. Long's Graham Rieska

2 packages active dry yeast
½ cup lukewarm water
4 cups milk, scalded and cooled
4 teaspoons salt

¼ cup lard or butter, melted
2 cups graham (coarse whole wheat) flour
6 to 7 cups bread flour

In a large bowl, soften the yeast in the warm water. Let stand 5 minutes until yeast begins to foam. Add the cooled milk, salt, and lard or butter. Stir in the graham flour until mixture is very smooth. Cover and let rise for 10 to 15 minutes until the mixture is puffy. Stir in the bread flour a cup at a time until the dough is smooth and stretchy.

Grease two large cookie sheets and sprinkle with a small amount of flour. Turn half of the dough out onto each of the two pans. With floured hands, flatten out to about 1-inch thickness. Let rise for an hour until puffy.

Preheat the oven to 375°F. With a fork, pierce the loaves all over. Bake for 35 to 40 minutes until loaves are browned. Cool on a rack.

Makes 2 free-form loaves

Christmas Trees

The Christmas season for us was marked by the beginning of Christmas tree season in October. Isä had discovered that he could make a bunch of money by cutting and selling Christmas trees. He would pile the cut trees onto the platform of his truck and deliver the trees to a Christmas tree lot in Minneapolis. In spite of his lack of education, Isä had also figured out how to make paint for flocking smaller Christmas trees that he would deliver along with the larger trees. He studied college-grade chemistry books and ordered the ingredients to make a paint that adhered to the three- to four-foot trees, which were actually the tops of larger balsam and spruce trees. The remainder of the trees were harvested later in the year as pulpwood.

Isä would flock the little trees with a fluffy substance after dipping them into all shades of blue, green, pink, and red paint. This preserved the trees

My father, Isä, in 1954.

Isä unloads Christmas trees in Minneapolis for the "Wise Men," circa 1948. My sisters Marion and Lillian are on the running board of the truck.

so that they didn't lose their needles as quickly as fresh trees. The colored, flocked trees were packed into narrow boxes that he would pile on his flatbed truck and haul to Minneapolis to ready and eager customers.

All I remember is that the lot was run by a group called the "Wise Men's Club." Later I came to realize that the name was actually the "Y's Men's Club"—the men who ran the YMCA in south Minneapolis. They were professional men who dressed well and knew that my dad enjoyed his booze. So they provided it. The hired men who accompanied my dad were always willing to make the trip with him because of that.

The Wise Men's Club, knowing we were a large family, sent us Christmas gifts every year, beautifully wrapped and transported in big plastic bags.

Pulla People

Mummy used to make little yeast-raised dough people for us at Christmastime. We called them gingerbread men—but of course, they weren't cookies and they didn't include any ginger. On top of it all, she didn't have a gingerbread man cookie cutter, so she used her all-purpose kitchen knife to slash pieces of dough to shape the legs, arms, and heads of these cute doughboys and doughgirls. Of course, if you have a large gingerbread boy cutter, use it! This dough is easy to handle because it is chilled, and chilled dough is really fun to work with!

2 packages active dry yeast
1 cup warm water (105°F to 115°F)
½ cup (1 stick) melted butter
½ cup sugar
3 large eggs
1 teaspoon salt
1 teaspoon freshly ground cardamom (optional)
4 to 4½ cups all-purpose flour
1 egg, beaten, for glaze
Raisins for eyes, noses, mouths, and buttons

In a large bowl, combine the yeast and warm water. Let stand for 5 minutes or until the yeast foams up. Stir in the butter, sugar, eggs, salt, and cardamom, if used. Gradually stir in 4 cups of the flour, 1 cup at a time, until the dough is too stiff to mix by hand (which may be before all 4 cups are added). Cover with plastic and refrigerate at least 2 hours or up to 4 days.

They were always a surprise. There were sweaters, coloring books, crayons, dolls for the girls, and little cars and trucks for the boys. But when Isä came home, regardless of the bags of gifts, it was another story. After his happy trip to Minneapolis, the homecoming wasn't so happy. Mummy had been left with the farm chores all day (and sometimes all night) and could hardly have been called a happy camper. She was "pissed," as we would say today. I knew how much he had had to drink when I observed him take that first step out of the truck. The memory, to this day, makes my heart thump, though I have tried hard to understand both sides of the story.

Lightly grease a baking sheet or cover it with parchment paper. Dust the dough with flour and turn out onto a lightly floured surface. Roll with a rolling pin or flatten with the palms of your hand until the dough is about 1 inch thick. With a large gingerbread boy cookie cutter, cut out people shapes and place on the prepared pan.

Or, cut the dough into 12 equal rectangles. Roll each part into a 6- by 3-inch rectangle. With the tip of a knife or with scissors, cut out snips of dough where the neck would be, to shape the head of each. Then, to shape the arms, make cuts about 1 inch lower than the neck, making the cuts on opposite sides of the body. With fingers, smooth out the body of the dough person. Starting from the center of the bottom of the dough, make a 3-inch slash to shape the legs. Place on the prepared pan, separating the legs slightly so they will not bake together. Roll one of the little snips of dough into a round shape for the head. Make a little hole where the dough person's nose would be and place a raisin in the hole. Roll out the other snip of dough into a skinny strand and place it over the top of the head to make hair. Repeat with the other dough parts to shape a total of 12 people.

Let rise, covered, for 45 minutes or until puffy.

Preheat the oven to 350°F. Brush the dough people with egg glaze; then press raisins into the dough to make the eyes, mouths, and buttons down the front of each. Bake for 12 to 15 minutes or until light golden brown. Remove from the pans and cool on a wire rack.

Makes 12 pulla people

Some Stories Are Hard to Tell

This is a story that's hard to tell, mainly because I saw it from the beginning to the end. It's not that we were so unusual, but in the end, love prevailed. The undying love of Mummy for my father and for our family has left us with a memory and a feeling that don't go away. It's as if Mummy is still with us—and she influenced not just our family but many others.

We all loved our Isä so much, even though he had a problem that plagued many in his family. His older brother, John, was an alcoholic who never recovered from his addiction. John had married Mummy's sister Helen and fathered two of my cousins before they were divorced. He was such a determined drunk that he was hard to contain even in the rural county-run nursing home where he spent his last days, escaping several times and making it to Floodwood to the infamous "liquor store" where fellow alcoholics gave him what he needed and wanted. He lived well into his eighties.

Isä might have had the same fate if it wouldn't have been for Mummy. Her profound love for him made her reject all advisers who recommended that she just "let him go."

At one point Mummy got Isä committed to Hazelden, an alcoholic treatment center in Minnesota. He thought it was a wonderful place. He met all kinds of important people there—doctors, lawyers, professors, and even priests, and that vindicated him.

Isä's love for "the bottle" was a source of both anger and entertainment for the family. I remember the boys, Rudy and Eugene especially, finding his hidden booze, emptying the bottles, peeing into them, and placing them back into their hiding spot. Isä was stuck because he couldn't reprimand them, and that delighted the boys.

It was a source of laughter to see him stagger around at a wedding reception, finishing off the champagne left by guests. It was after one of those episodes that he realized he couldn't walk if he had even so much as a drop of drink. He decided to call it quits, and it was during the last couple of years of his life that he decided he couldn't handle alcohol at all anymore. He died at the age of eighty-eight.

Mummy at the wheel of the joker with my aunt Helen in back, circa 1950. Lillian is holding her doll, and Rudy and Eugene look on.

I have a photo that shows Mummy driving the joker, the converted Model A we used for farm chores. It was the only vehicle available to her. She was determined to go the four miles into town to "get" Isä and bring him home. I took a photo with my Brownie camera.

Vesala

Vesala was always an old man to us as kids, although in reality he was only in his forties or fifties at the time. He lived on a homestead adjoining our farm. It wasn't until I was much older that I came to know he even had a first name. It was the custom of Finns to call each other by their last name. So, Jussi (John) Vesala was always just "Vesala" to us.

Vesala had the reputation of being a stingy old miser who mistrusted the banks and kept his money in jars buried in his field. When he needed help—as he often did—he would hire my younger brothers, and he paid them well, peeling off paper bills from musty rolls of dollars he unearthed from his secret places in the field. They would run home and laugh and cheer as they passed the money around for everyone to smell.

Vesala had two horses that he used for his fieldwork, and he grew award-winning oats and potatoes. On quiet summer days we could hear him singing to his horses in low, mournful notes.

Although many would have called him a little strange, Mummy always welcomed him into the house when he appeared at the door. He never knocked to announce his arrival, but we could smell him. Salty, sweaty, reeking of wood smoke and burned coffee, he seemed to leave his stench everywhere. However, a more loyal neighbor could never be found. Whenever we needed help he was there.

When I was sixteen years old, Mummy and Isä decided to take a trip "out west" to visit my aunt Elma and uncle Mal. I was left to take care of the farm and the "little kids," and Vesala came in the evening to help feed and milk the cows. At that point I was perfectly capable of doing the chores, but it was a comfort to have him there.

When Vesala came to visit, he just walked in and sat down at the table. We would always try to see how many pieces of buttered korppua (dry toast or zwieback) or cinnamon rolls he could eat. We piled them as high as we could on a plate, and he always finished off all of them—along with mugs of coffee sweetened and mixed with milk.

In the fall, Vesala would often buy a dozen eggs from Mummy. He insisted on paying for them, as he was too proud to accept them for free. One spring he came over to complain to Mummy that one of the eggs was rotten. That was not a surprise to her, as he had no refrigerator and he had had the eggs a good six months! She immediately replaced the egg with a fresh one. There were so many funny moments with Vesala. One time when he came to visit, we were looking at the Montgomery Ward catalog. Mummy jested to him that "look, you could order yourself a really good-looking wife," pointing at dress models. Vesala hemmed and hawed, he looked up at the ceiling and at the walls, scratched his head, and finally replied in Finnish: "If I got a wife, then I'd have to get a cow, too."

Another time, Vesala walked the four miles into Floodwood to buy his bread and ring bologna at the Co-op store. I happened to be working at the store when he toddled in with two backpacks. When I offered to put his groceries into one of the packs, he said, "No, not that one. It has lice in it."

One summer, Vesala came over to announce that he was leaving America and going back to his native Finland, to the farm called Vesala from which he got his name. Mummy offered to help him wash his clothes for the trip and pack his suitcase. He arrived a day or so later with a gunnysack stuffed with the clothes he wanted to take along. Mummy washed and ironed them, and even offered him a cap that Isä had discarded because he had a new one. He took his sweat-encrusted cap and pitched it over the fence as he accepted his welcome gift. He left Duluth with his clean clothes packed in a Northrup King gunnysack slung over his shoulder.

As it turned out, Vesala found his home farm, but nobody he knew lived there anymore and all his relatives were gone. The owners gave him a sauna and a bunk in one of the outbuildings, where he could live while he worked on the farm as a hired hand.

He called my mother and said he wanted to come back to Minnesota because there was nobody in Finland whom he knew anymore. But he was not allowed to come back to the United States, as he had never taken out citizenship and was now "too old" to be allowed back into the country.

Dick and I happened to be in Helsinki at the time when he told us this story. He had carried his life savings in his overall pockets, wrapped in rolls like he did when he buried them in his field. He asked us to find him the cheapest room we could in Helsinki, and when he pulled out his thick roll of one-hundred-dollar bills, the eyes of the manager of the "YMCA" popped out and he warned Vesala to be very careful!

The last time we saw this independent old man he was toddling across the busiest intersection of trams in Helsinki. He died of natural causes somewhere in the city.

Floodwood, My Hometown

Floodwood is a quiet, innocent town and when I was growing up, there were three general stores, a post office, a couple of filling stations, and a few little "ma and pa" businesses. All three of the general stores carried groceries, some dry goods, and a few hardware and farm supplies. Hill's Mercantile was the "fanciest" of them and perhaps the most stylish—if anything in Floodwood in the 1930s was stylish. Ylitalo's was a smaller store and was owned by a family of Finns. We did most of our shopping at the Co-op store, owned by a cooperative—again, mostly Finns. The Co-op had a garage, too, that sold Fords. Shipley's garage sold Chevrolets. It was a small town, and we knew what we could get where. I could identify which store things came from by the smell of the stuff in the shopping bag. Each store was unique.

Across the street from Hill's was the First State Bank, a neat block of a building with windows you could not see into. Tillie and Jack Rosendahl Sr. owned the bank. I was later offered a "good paying" job at the bank after graduating from high school but turned it down, much to my parents' regret, because I planned to go to the University of Minnesota. It seems nobody expected a farm girl whose parents lacked "deep pockets" to have such high-falutin ideas.

I was awarded a one-hundred-dollar scholarship from the University of Minnesota Duluth that would be renewed each of the four years I attended and that covered my tuition and fees. I worked three jobs on campus to pay for my room and board.

Isä always did all of the shopping in Floodwood, so Mummy kept a slip of paper on which she wrote things that were needed and for Isä to buy on his next trip into town. I remember the time when we had a plugged-up sewer pipe and Mummy wrote on the slip "sewer diggers," as she didn't know what to call the tool you'd use to clean out the sewer. Isä came home with a pair of tweezers. He hadn't been able to figure out what she had written on the slip. He had consulted with several clerks at the store, trying to make out what she had written. The best they could figure out is that she had written "sliver diggers," and so he came home with the tweezers.

Ylitalo's store was the closest to the school. We had an hour break for lunch, and often I was assigned the duty of buying something that we needed at home. One day I needed to buy myself a yellow pencil. I noticed that the pencils were marked "2 for 5 cents" so I asked the clerk, "How much is one pencil?" The answer was "three cents." "Well," I replied, "I'll take the two-cent one." I guess I was cheap even in the first grade. My mother entered this exchange in a "bright sayings" contest she heard about on the radio and won a five-pound tub of "Lan-o-Sheen" soap. I can't remember if I got the pencil for two or three cents.

Main Street in Floodwood stretched from Ylitalo's store to Hill's Mercantile. Across the corner from Ylitalo's was the pool hall—a place to be avoided. Then came the post office, where we had to go to pick up mail and our newspaper.

How the Bible Chapel earned a place on Main Street was never disclosed. It was the church of bible-thumping preachers and summertime "revivals." Across from the Bible Chapel was Koskela's Café. Sam Koskela made sandwiches, simmered soup, and offered short-order breakfasts and burgers. It was a hangout for farmers. The story goes that somebody entered the café one morning and asked Sam what kind of pie he had that day. His response, "I have two kinds of pie, socklat cake, and donuts!"

Just past Wester's garage was the Rexall drugstore where we filled prescriptions and bought cough medicine, cosmetics, combs, and other sundries. It was a favorite gathering place for schoolkids. On the right as you entered was a long counter with stools, and from the fountain they served root beer floats and sundaes of all kinds. The air had the smell of chemicals and perfume. The sundaes were made with ice cream from the Floodwood Creamery—the same place that picked up the milk from our farm every day.

When it came to shopping for clothes, it was always best to wait until we took the long trip to Duluth, where you could find anything you wanted or needed. I'd shop at Three Sisters on Superior Street, or Freimuth's or Oreck's or even Glass Block. But shopping trips like that were few and far between.

One year, when I was around thirteen, the end-of-the-school-year picnic was coming up and I needed a bathing suit. The picnic was scheduled to be held at the beach in the community park situated on the Floodwood River bank (sometimes called the BAB). I searched all of the stores in Floodwood for a bathing suit, without any luck. In a last-ditch effort, I tried Rahja's clothing store, even though they sold mainly men's stuff. Old Man Rahja held up a pair of men's swimming trunks and declared, "Sorry, I don't have any women's bathing suits, but you could wear tis and a prassiere," he said in his heavy Finnish accent, rolling the r's. Humiliated, I left the store as fast as I could. Mummy said, "He was only trying to be helpful!"

Highway 2 went diagonally just on the outskirts of town. That's where the gas stations were and a small wayside café called Larson's that served

Sam's Socklat Cake

This is a simple chocolate cake made with Hershey's cocoa—a rare treat for farmers who dropped into Sam Koskela's café, which they did more for the conversation than for the coffee and a treat. Sam's wife baked a fresh cake each morning in a large, rectangular pan, and she would spread it with her own homemade fudge frosting. When we made this cake at home we called it "boiling water" chocolate cake. Others call it "one-bowl chocolate cake."

1¾ cups sugar
1¾ cups all-purpose flour
¾ cup unsweetened cocoa powder
1½ teaspoons baking powder
1½ teaspoons baking soda
½ teaspoon salt
2 eggs
1 cup milk
½ cup (1 stick) butter, melted, or ½ cup vegetable oil
2 teaspoons real vanilla extract
1 cup boiling water

Heat oven to 350°F. Grease a 9- by 13-inch rectangular baking pan.

Stir together sugar, flour, cocoa, baking powder, baking soda, and salt in large bowl. Add eggs, milk, melted butter or oil, and vanilla; beat on medium speed of mixer 2 minutes or, as my mother would say, "beat like crazy." Stir in boiling water (batter will be thin). Pour batter into prepared pan.

Bake 35 to 40 minutes or until wooden pick inserted in center comes out clean. Cool completely before topping with frosting.

Makes 12 servings

Chocolate Cocoa Fudge Frosting

In a saucepan, combine 1 stick butter and ⅔ cup unsweetened cocoa. Place over medium heat, stirring until the butter is melted and cocoa is perfectly blended in.

Add 3 cups sifted powdered sugar alternately with milk until frosting is of spreading consistency. Add 1 teaspoon vanilla and again, "Beat like crazy!" Spread cooled frosting over the cooled cake.

passersby and Saturday night drunks. When I turned sixteen I got a weekend job as a waitress at the café. A long counter separated me from the stools where inebriated old men would slobber over their coffee cups and call out for more—calling me unsavory names as well. The smell of deep-fried potatoes, mixed with the men's alcohol-soaked breath, cigarettes, burned coffee, the scream of the jukebox, and the chill of the evening made me realize this wasn't a career for me.

Then, there was Two-Buck Millie who loved to entertain gentlemen who probably were not so gentle. They would call to her from across Main Street and she would respond either with an invitation or with "Got the rag on, honey, but call me next week and I'll show you a good time."

Yes, I grew up in a quiet, innocent town.

Lincoln School in Floodwood

A piece of me died when I visited the school of my childhood a couple of years ago, the school I attended from grade one to high school graduation. Oh, the new school is lovely, efficient, and modern, and so much more attuned to the needs of today's students. But I missed the old one.

In the school of my youth, there were three round windows in each classroom's art deco wooden door. The windows were positioned one above the other, so that even the shortest child could peer in from the lowest window. Those windows appear in my dreams from time to time. The hallway floors were of a solid material, not asphalt tiles, and they were polished to a bright sheen. At the beginning of the school year, the whole school smelled of wax and fresh varnish.

On the first level at the end of one hallway was the first-grade room with its faint smell of crayons, paper, and tempera paints mixed with the mint of white wintergreen–flavored library paste. Some kids used to eat the library paste. I never did. The ceilings were high and the huge double-hung windows could be opened to let in fresh air.

For all of my twelve years at the Lincoln School in Floodwood, Adelaide Orr was the fourth-grade teacher. She had a barrel-like stature with skinny legs and hair pulled back into a bun. The bad boys used to chant a naughty rhyme about her: "Old Lady Orr, shit on the floor and wiped her ass on the knob of the door." I wonder if she ever knew about that little jingle. I could never repeat it myself; in fact, it was hard even to write it down—but it is a part of history. I had trouble visualizing the scene.

There was one especially outstanding teacher at the Floodwood School—Tom Riley. He was tall and bony and combed his charcoal-gray hair straight back. He wore big thick glasses that sat on his long, straight nose and magnified his eyes

Mr. Riley was my favorite teacher. Not because he was especially nice to me, but because I really learned a lot from him. He taught chemistry and physics and explained things so clearly that I could really visualize what he was saying. The laws of physics seemed so sensible after he explained them.

"For every force, there is an equal and opposite force," he'd practically

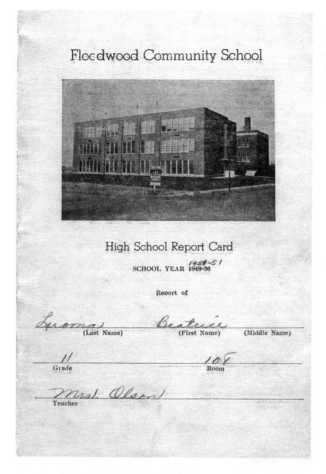

Floodwood Community School, where I spent every grade until heading to Duluth for college.

shout. Then he went on to explain how you could balance any two bodies on a teeter-totter by placing the heavier one nearer the center.

I remember memorizing the periodic table. Not because I was supposed to, but because it hung in the front of the classroom—a large poster with colorful squared-off blocks, each with the symbol of all the elements from which the entire world is made.

"Oxygen (O) loves hydrogen (H), so much that one oxygen can connect with two hydrogens to make water," he said. "So the formula for water is H_2O." I pictured oxygen holding hands with two hydrogens as they walked down a path.

The whole school had only one movie projector and it seemed it was never working the way it should. *Call Riley!* Mr. Riley would come into the class-room and do something to the projector, and would always make it work.

The Rileys were staunch Catholics. His wife, Del, was proud of her heritage and could trace her relations back to the Revolutionary War. She was, in fact, a member of the Daughters of the American Revolution. Her husband, however, never bothered to trace his heritage. In his words, "Hell, they probably hung half of them!"

The school had a gymnasium where all our important gatherings were held, as well as basketball games, plays, and even graduation ceremonies. In the winter our physical education classes were held in that gym. The room had huge pillars at least three feet in diameter. One day we were playing a game called "crack the whip," and I was at the end of the "whip." You were supposed to hang on tight to the next player. I went flying into one of those pillars, and instead of cracking the whip, I cracked my collarbone!

Thinking of that gymnasium and the stage brings back the memory of the tragic death of one of my classmates in a hunting accident. It was traumatic because it was the first time I had experienced the death of somebody I knew well. I was probably in fifth grade. His funeral was held in the gymnasium. The old gym shows up often in my dreams. The hymn "My Faith Looks Up to Thee" always conjures up the deep emotion of this first loss of a friend in a terrible accident.

There was also the home economics classroom, which was the site of the 4-H demonstration competitions every summer. The room held the faint smell of onions, spices, and cooking, though the kitchen was always sparkling clean and had that "neat and put away" look to it.

The school in those days didn't have a parking lot for anything but the half dozen big yellow buses that backed up side by side to load and unload kids. Kids didn't have cars until many years later. Those who lived in town walked to school and us country kids rode the bus. If I missed the bus I had to walk four miles along back roads to get home. This didn't happen often. But when it did, there were always interesting things to see along the way. I'd walk along Highway 8 across the bridge over the St. Louis River, past the Tahjas' farm, then to the corner and past the Dahlbackas' place. Then, past the Jensens' and on to the next corner. To the right there was the Matalamakis' farm, then on the other side of the road the Baileys' farm. After that it was about another three-quarters of a mile to an intersection that we called "four corners." A family of skunks lived in that stretch, and I had to be careful not to disturb them.

Four corners was often the place where the big yellow school bus picked us up when the roads were muddy. Spring air. I loved the smell of wet mud, the aroma of new leaves on the poplar trees—and the unmistakable aroma

Outside our house on the way to school, circa 1948. On my right in the back is Marion, and our sisters Betty Mae (left) and Lillian are in front.

of new buds on the balsams. One mile more to get home and sometimes I'd just drag myself along enjoying the countryside. I'd walk to the "blueberry corner" remembering the fall when the blueberries were so abundant that we could "milk" them into our pails. Then on to Faegre's corner, and I'd at last turn down onto our driveway—the quarter mile rimmed by the very pine trees that Isä had planted. It was at this corner that I could smell when Mummy had baked bread. Ahh, the aroma!

When the school bus dropped us off at that corner, at the end of that driveway, the aroma of fresh-baked bread gave us the incentive to run home. There on the counter of the kitchen would be the fat, round loaves, propped up against each other as they cooled. Mummy would order us to hold off on the bread until suppertime, or else we wouldn't have an appetite. On more than one occasion we would dig a hole through the back crust of a loaf and pull out the warm puffs of bread until the loaf was nothing but a buttered shell.

Anne Brown's Beauty Parlor

All the time I was growing up I had naturally stick-straight hair. Thick, stubborn, and hard to curl. For special occasions—like the monthly "services" at Uncle Frank's—Mummy used a curling iron to coax my hair into curls. We heated the curling iron in the chimney of our kerosene lamp. One had to be very careful not to touch the scalp with the hot iron, as that could result in serious burns. It was a touchy and time-consuming operation.

The style when I was in school was curly hair, and so a couple of times a year I would get a permanent. It wasn't anything I really looked forward to because it hurt. It hurt a lot. Anne Brown had set up a beauty parlor in her house that faced downtown Floodwood.

Showing off my curly hair in 1939. I'm five years old, Leonard is four, and our mother is holding Marion, age two.

After a shampoo, when Anne would scrub the daylights out of my scalp, she would take a strand of hair at a time and wipe a stinky solution onto the strand. Then she would wrap it tightly around a curler. It would feel like all of my hair strands were being pulled out of my head at once.

Anne twisted about fifty curlers onto my head, all wrapped with my hair, and clamp onto each curler something that had a long cord that extended to a heater and applied heat to my hair. I had to tell her if something got too hot, and she would use a blower to cool off that spot. There often were spots on my scalp that suffered burns. The process required stamina—almost like going to the dentist's office—but I really wanted curly hair, so I made myself withstand the torture.

I didn't want to complain to Anne because I knew what she was doing was necessary for the outcome. But it did hurt. Then she would calmly say, "You have to suffer to be beautiful!" My hair would be really frizzy curly at first, but after about two weeks it would tame down to be a nice, smooth wave. It was all worth it!

I have always thought it would be great to learn how to use makeup—especially to make my little eyes bigger. First, I thought you had to be old enough to use makeup. Then I wondered at what point would I be old enough? I still haven't felt old enough to put on eye shadow, eyeliner, and eyebrow pencil. When I tried it once, a friend looked at me, shocked, and asked, "What happened to your eyes?" I guess I looked like I had been in a fight and lost.

Town Kids versus Country Kids

I was a country kid. I worked in the field. I shoveled manure. I rode the bus to school. I smelled like barn when I got to school. I guess I didn't even know—or care—to envy those who were privileged to be able to walk to school every day. I wore hand-me-downs from "rich" people in Duluth. I was perfectly happy with my lot in life. My home was a beautiful place with woods and streams and wildflowers and wild strawberries. We had a great rhythm of life—work all week, clean house on Saturdays, and then enjoy the fresh smell of clean sheets and feel squeaky clean after sauna.

When I got to the age when I was dating, I found kids with similar values, not in Floodwood, but in towns like Meadowlands and Toivola that were a few miles away on Highway 73. I dated a boy named Floyd when I was fifteen years old. Our relationship was purely platonic, but we had so much fun together and with the gang of country kids who were all so full of crazy ideas.

Floyd and the gang would pick me up on a typical Saturday night, and we'd go to the show (movie) in Floodwood, and then with six of us in his Buick, we'd drive back to Meadowlands to have a glass of milk and a glazed doughnut at Berweger's Café. Sometimes, just for the fun of it, the boys would put a two-quart bottle of 7Up in a creek to chill, midway between Floodwood and Meadowlands. We'd stop and all drink from that bottle. What fun!

One year, around 1950, the tent caterpillar outbreak was huge and the roads were covered with swarms of the wriggling worms. Not only that, they crawled up the walls of homes and filled ditches. They made country roads so slippery that when you slammed on the brakes, the car would slide from one side to another.

The guys would dare each other to eat the worms. Floyd, of course, did and earned his daredevil crown. Country kid macho! Us girls would squeal with disgust.

One Saturday evening, when Floyd showed up, his face was lobster red. He explained that he had had a contest with the hired men on his father's farm to see who could stand the largest number of ladles of water on the hot sauna stove. (Remember, Finns always take a sauna on Saturday evening.) Each ladle of water thrown onto the hot rocks produces an incredible swoosh of steam. Although the temperature of the room goes down, the steam makes it feel hotter. Floyd won the battle. Who says country kids can't have fun?

Country Carrot Meatloaf

Meatloaf was a standard dish in our home and is still one of my favorite things to have on hand for snacks, sandwiches, and other quick meals. When we had ground venison, we used that. Later, on a graduate student's budget, I devised this recipe to "extend" the meat while adding a vegetable too—grated carrots actually added not just flavor and nutrition to the meatloaf, but succulent moistness, too.

1 cup bread crumbs, made from 2 slices firm homemade bread
¾ cup milk
2 large carrots, shredded
1 medium onion, finely chopped
2½ pounds lean ground beef, venison, or bison
3 eggs
1 tablespoon salt
¼ teaspoon pepper

For the glaze

¼ cup catsup
3 tablespoons brown sugar
2 tablespoons prepared mustard

Preheat the oven to 350°F.

In a large bowl, combine the bread crumbs and milk. Add the carrots, onion, beef, eggs, salt, and pepper.

With an electric hand mixer, or by hand, which takes longer, mix all of the ingredients well. Pat into a 9- by 5-inch loaf pan.

In a small bowl, mix the catsup, brown sugar, and mustard well and spread evenly over the top of the meatloaf. Bake, uncovered, for 1 to 1½ hours.

Makes 8 servings

Seeds for a Bible

I had so many questions about the meaning of life, and at a tender age I had come to believe that the Bible would hold all the answers. Since the only Bible we had in the house was in Finnish, it was my mission to get a Bible of my very own, one that I could read and study.

One day, when I was eleven years old, I was reading a magazine and came across an ad placed by a seed company: "You can earn rewards by selling seeds."

One of the rewards for selling a certain amount of seeds was a Holy Bible. Wow! I knew I could do that. So I signed up for the deal. It wasn't long before I received a package in the mail with packets of vegetable and flower seeds. I can't remember how much they sold for, or how many I had to sell to gain enough points to "win" a Bible.

When the seeds arrived, I piled them into my bicycle basket and started down the road. Selling has never been easy for me—in fact, I like to joke that I couldn't sell ice cream in hell! But sell them I did, all the same.

When I had sold just enough seeds to turn in the right number of points, I "won" a Bible. I just couldn't wait for it to arrive. When it did, my name, Beatrice Luoma, was imprinted in gold on the right-hand corner of its black leather cover. My own Bible!

I fingered through the pages and filled in what I could of the family register that divided the Old and New Testaments. Here I would later record the deaths of my grandfather Joel Honkala and grandmother Sanna Luoma. I didn't fill in any more pages until my marriage to Richard Ojakangas on Sunday, June 10, 1956, and the births of my children, Catherine Lee Ojakangas on October 1, 1957, and Gregory Wayne Ojakangas on August 14, 1959. After that, I retired my King James Version in favor of the newer translations.

One page of my new Bible was titled "Forty questions answered in the Word of God." The intriguing questions covered a wide range of topics, but the one that really seemed important was "What is the greatest sin of all?" I was absolutely sure it had something to do with sex. But what was the answer? I was surprised when I read that the greatest sin was not to believe in

God. This was, of course, written in the King James Version—even today a bit difficult to interpret. This sin is referred to in 1 John 5:10 ("He that believeth on the Son of God hath the witness in himself; he that believeth not in God hath made him a liar, because he believeth not the record that God gave of his son"), the Gospel according to John 5:38, and Numbers 23:19.

"Hmph," I thought. "This doesn't tell me anything I didn't know!"

Heaven and How to Get There

I was fourteen and my sister Marion was ten. We were representing our family at our neighbors' church—the Floodwood Bible Chapel—at their annual "spiritual revival" campaign. Our neighbors had come to our confirmations and baptisms in the Lutheran church, and our parents thought it was only right that somebody from our family reciprocate and attend our neighbors' "important event."

The little white wooden church sat right in the middle of town, next to the post office and across the street from Koskela's Café. It looked friendly enough, though not particularly inviting. When the front door opened, people streamed into the church.

Marion and I sat about halfway back in the center of the pew, thinking we could hide within the crowd. Stretched across the front of the church just below the ceiling was a banner that read in big block letters, "HEAVEN AND HOW TO GET THERE."

The preacher stood tall in the center of the stage, hair slicked back. He had a big mouthful of teeth and when he launched into his message it was directed, we thought, right at the two of us. We cringed.

The neighbor lady nodded her approval. Her family agreed. After all, her kids had been told not to associate with us because we were sinners. They had heard that we went to movies and school dances and played Old Maid with cards. We went to the carnival when it was in town. Isä had bought a television when they were first available, much to their unvoiced disapproval. Plus, our father was known to drink too much and our mother was always pregnant. To top it off, we were Finns. Heathens.

They probably thought they would help us out by taking at least a couple of us to their revival meeting. Maybe we could be saved.

It was a hot July day in Minnesota. The men and boys were wearing loose white shirts and their Sunday-best pants. The women, in their long, printed dresses, scarves, and Cuban-heeled shoes with black socks, responded with "Yes, yes" as the preacher became more and more emphatic.

"You!" he suddenly pointed at us. "You need to be saved! You need to be born again! Come forward—be saved!" We wondered what he meant. Saved from what?

Marion and I looked at each other quizzically, while the crowd around us nodded and swayed. It was getting pretty warm.

"Now," said the preacher, "I'll sing a song for you!"

The piano was backed up to the wall on the left side of the stage. He pulled out the bench, craned his neck toward the assembly, and clanked out a couple of chords. Then he launched into a nasaly rendition of a praise-and-glory song. The congregation joined in. They knew all the words. A few started toward the front of the sanctuary, somewhat entranced.

"Come and be saved!"

When he pronounced his final benediction "See you in the morning of the glory land!" we knew one thing for sure—we were getting out of there as soon as we could, even if we had to walk the four miles home.

Confirmation in the Finnish Lutheran Church

Sitting around a table with a cup of coffee today, my friends and I often exchange our confirmation stories. Some of my friends grew up in churches other than Lutheran and never were confirmed. In the Lutheran church, confirmation is considered simply an affirmation of our baptism—and not a "rite of passage." At least that is what I have come to believe. When I grew up, it was after confirmation that one was considered an adult in the church and could receive communion, the Eucharist, or the Lord's Supper.

Preparing for confirmation for me and my Finnish friends in Floodwood consisted of two weeks of classes in the summertime. I biked into town each day with my Bible and confirmation books in the basket of my blue Schwinn two-wheeler. I loved my Bible history book. It had a pinkish-orange cover and had a wonderful new-book aroma.

There are three phrases from my confirmation days that have stuck with me all my life. Three phrases that actually have little to do with the building of faith—or the opposite. These three phrases remind me of my heritage, of the bit of humor I grew up with, and of a wonderful relationship with the church. I credit this to Pastor Könönen, who preached in Finnish and had limited English.

He would start our lessons each day with a few of his limited English phrases. I don't remember the order but one of them was, "I vonce had opportunity," after which he would trail off into Finnish. Another was, "It is my obligation . . . ," again lapsing into Finnish, and the third was, "I have gum [come] to the conclusion . . ."

We never did know what his opportunities, his obligations, or his conclusions were, but the phrases give me a little inward chuckle when I think of them.

My friend Joyce, a fellow confirmand, and I would address each other with, "Have you come to any conclusions lately?" Or, "Have you had any opportunities recently?" Or, "Do you have any obligations today?"

These remembrances might not seem very faith inspiring, but to me they fix my memories in a positive way to my confirmation days.

Confirmation Day in 1949 with my friends: Joyce is on the left, Beatrice is in the middle, and I am on the right.

My special white confirmation dress had a delicious texture: it was made of a white piqué with a white lace inset at the yoke. I wore that dress only once. The day after my confirmation we packaged it up and sent it to relatives in Finland who had very limited resources (the Finnish–Russian war had just ended). A second cousin wore the same dress for her confirmation in Kurikka, Finland. We sent other things, too: coffee, sugar, nylons, cotton socks, even shoes. I could say that opportunity, obligation, and conclusions also were sent with the package.

Till the Cows Come Home

It was 1950. I was one month short of my sixteenth birthday when my parents planned to take a road trip "out west" to visit Elma and Mal Berg, my mother's oldest sister and her husband, who lived in Eugene, Oregon. Isä had bought a brand-new 1950 Ford for the trip. I was left at home to take care of the farm. Alvin and Nancy went to stay with Aunt Esther and Uncle John. Rudy and Eugene went to stay with Aunt Helen. That left Marion, age thirteen, Leonard, age fourteen, and me to take care of the farm.

They left on June 6, and mid-June was about the best time to leave for two weeks. School was out. The crops had been planted and the weather was nice. The cows were in full milk, and they had arranged for Vesala (our bachelor neighbor who lived on the next forty) to come and help out with the milking. I don't remember, but another neighbor, Lloyd Fagre, might have been on our call list for help if we needed it.

I knew the drill. Up and into the barn by 5:00 A.M. after a quick cup of coffee. The cows entered the barn, each filing into her favorite spot. (I often think how much like a cow I am—always selecting the same chair in choir today.) We scooped a measure of feed—"middlings," a combination of coarsely ground grains—into the trough in front of each cow. Once a week they got a portion of soybean meal as well, to keep their coats shiny. The soybean meal was finely ground and I thought it was delicious too. We kept it in a large bin in the barn and I'd grab a handful as a personal treat. I thought it tasted a little like peanut butter.

We didn't have milking machines at the time, so Marion, Leonard, and I milked our share of the cows by hand, four or five cows each. The fresh milk had to be strained into ten-gallon cans, after which the full cans were lifted into the cooling tank in the milk house. A full ten-gallon can weighed about a hundred pounds, so it was a two-person job to lift each one into the cooling tank that was in the milk house, separate from the barn. The cooling tank was a rectangular box made of cement and filled with cold water that we hand-pumped from the well. We usually filled two ten-gallon cans with each milking.

As each cow was relieved of her milk, she was turned out of the barn into the pasture behind the barn to drink from the creek and graze in the field.

When the milking was done—usually at seven in the morning and seven at night—I felt free until the cows would come home again, their heavy bags swinging as they entered the barn.

Later in the morning the "milk man" drove into the farm with a big truck and picked up the cans that he then delivered to the creamery in Floodwood.

I have on my dresser to this day a little wooden box with the picture of the four presidents on Mount Rushmore. It was the gift Mummy and Isä brought home for me from their trip out west. I don't remember what the gifts were for the others, but I have kept that little box all these years. In it I have stored my recognition pins from 4-H, the National Honor Society, and from my years in the Floodwood High School band—these were the pins that we would traditionally attach to our high school sweaters down along the neckband. I need to use a magnifying glass now to read the labels on them.

The End-of-Summer Prize

I joined the local 4-H club as an adolescent, not necessarily to learn to cook but because I wanted to win a trip to the State Fair. Still, I enrolled in one food-related project after another. Each came with a bulletin outlining basic important things to know and learn, along with a report form. The reports were such fun to write. I had to keep track of everything I prepared and cooked throughout the year. By the end of the year the report was so bulky it almost constituted a cookbook by itself!

Food preparation, food preservation, bread baking, canning, clothing construction, and dairy foods were among my favorite personal project choices. All of the projects were interesting to me, and I concentrated on them one at a time.

I entered in the food preparation category by planning food demonstrations to compete for a trip to the State Fair in August.

The first year, I offered a demonstration making an egg salad sandwich and an eggnog. During that first competition I learned two valuable lessons: always have "standby" ingredients, and be more prepared for probing questions by the judges. The first step of the competition started with the local clubs, proceeded to the county competition, and from there the possibility of winning that coveted trip to the State Fair.

Nervously, I lined up all of the ingredients for my sandwich and eggnog on a tray—slices of homemade bread, butter, a hard-cooked egg; milk, eggs, sugar, and vanilla for the eggnog. I had another tray holding the utensils that I would need. I was careful to plan for a space between the trays for my "show and tell." I tied my hair back and put on a clean apron, and when my turn came up, I nervously carried my trays to the counter in the home economics department of the Floodwood school where the local competition was always held.

Two judges—looking very official—sat in front of me with notepads and pens. At this point I realized how utterly unprepared I was. I picked up my single hard-cooked egg and cracked it open. The yolk bounced out of the white and rolled down the counter, over the edge, and onto the floor. I ran after it and plopped it into the bowl and continued with my demonstration. What I should have done is have another egg ready, and I could have explained just how that egg should have been cooked perfectly. I got a red ribbon on my demonstration, not good enough to proceed to the county competition. The following year I chose to demonstrate the making of cottage cheese. In fact, I even made my own version of a cheddar cheese by draining the cottage cheese, pressing it into a mold, and brining the finished product. That was good for a blue ribbon at the county fair—but still not good enough to win a trip to the State Fair.

With a year to contemplate my next attempt to win the end-of-summer prize, I chose to demonstrate my mother's favorite—a special chiffon cake that she made for every birthday or whenever we needed something special. Mummy loved to make chiffon cakes—she felt it was a "healthy" cake because it used so many eggs and a small amount of sugar. People always marveled at the flavor and texture of this cake that was seldom frosted, just dusted with a bit of powdered sugar. For variety, sometimes we would drizzle it with a thin powdered sugar icing. The cake is one that first appeared in a Betty Crocker leaflet and is still being published today. I worked on the recipe and when we didn't have oranges on hand, I'd make it with lemons.

In preparation for the next year's competition and attempt to win a trip to the State Fair, I learned as much as I could about the leavening properties, the sizes of eggs, how to properly separate the egg yolk from the whites, and how to whip the whites. Since we had a coop full of chickens we had no shortage of eggs. After baking cake after cake, I had the demonstration down so pat that I could practice the talking parts without actually making cakes. I needed to be so prepared that there would be no gaps in things to say as I whisked, stirred, and folded the batter in front of the judges and my friends. I made the orange-flavored spongy cake, but talked about all the different variations on the theme. There was no end to my jabbering—the more I learned, the more there was to talk about!

I practiced my demonstration all year: while milking cows, while pitching hay from the loft, and while shoveling manure from the gutters in the barn. Farmwork can be somewhat mindless physical labor, but when I had my demonstration to think about the work went quickly. I used to wonder if the cows had learned how to make a chiffon cake themselves after that year.

All summer long I baked cake after cake. We gave these cakes to friends and neighbors and still had enough for my dad and his hired workers. I made a cake for my ailing grandmother on her birthday in June 1950.

I even baked a cake for my friend, the other Beatrice in my school class. On her birthday I put the cake in the basket of my bicycle and pumped the eight miles to her home to present her with her birthday cake. Beatrice was the oldest child in her family and had four or five siblings. They lived in a

At the barn in 1949, likely practicing my 4-H demonstrations for the cows.

small two-room house and didn't have animals and gardens like we did. It was the only birthday cake she had that year.

Soon it was August and time to put my demonstration together. I carefully planned my presentation and reviewed all the information I had learned about cooking with eggs, their nutritional qualities and why eggs a couple of days old whipped up better than freshly laid ones, the kind of flour that is best to use in a cake, and why mixing techniques are so important. I described the "folding of whipped whites into the basic cake."

When I presented my demonstration at the South St. Louis County Fair in Proctor, I won the coveted trip to the Minnesota State Fair. It was all worth it.

At the State Fair in St. Paul that year we were housed in the 4-H building, where we were assigned to triple bunk beds and given tickets for three meals a day in the dining hall. After breakfast we headed out onto the fairgrounds to enjoy the special exhibits and food. Spudnuts—raised glazed doughnuts made with potato water as the base (hence the name)—cost a nickel and was the first booth we hit. We enjoyed one every day after as well. Then we'd hit the booth where we could drink all the free milk we wanted, another favorite. Machinery Hill, where all the cute boys hung out, was the most fun. We weren't fond of the Midway because it was too expensive, hot, and crowded, but the cattle barns, horticulture building, and all the other exhibit buildings consumed our time.

Practicing my 4-H bread project. I'm wearing a dress I made, and my friend Beverly is taking a loaf of fresh bread from the oven.

Ready for the South St. Louis County Fair!

Lemon or Orange Chiffon Cake

The basic chiffon cake is flavored with lemon or orange, rises into a spongy texture because of the beaten eggs, and is leavened also with baking powder. It's an interesting sponge type of cake that absorbs fruit juices beautifully, making it a great cake to serve with fresh berries or a juicy fruit—like pineapple.

2 cups all-purpose flour
1½ cups granulated sugar
3 teaspoons baking powder
1 teaspoon salt
¾ cup cold water
½ cup vegetable oil
2 teaspoons vanilla
2 teaspoons grated lemon or orange zest
7 egg yolks
1 cup egg whites (8 eggs)
½ teaspoon cream of tartar

Lemon Glaze

⅓ cup butter or margarine
2 cups powdered sugar
½ teaspoon grated lemon or orange zest
2 to 4 tablespoons hot lemon or orange juice

Move oven rack to lowest position. Heat oven to 325°F. In large bowl, mix flour, sugar, baking powder, and salt. Beat in cold water, oil, vanilla, lemon zest, and egg yolks until smooth.

In large bowl, beat egg whites and cream of tartar with electric mixer on high speed until stiff peaks form. Gradually pour egg yolk mixture over beaten egg whites, folding with rubber spatula just until blended. Pour into ungreased 10-inch angel food (tube) cake pan.

Bake about 1 hour 15 minutes or until top springs back when touched lightly. Immediately turn pan upside down onto heatproof funnel or bottle. Let hang until completely cool, about 2 hours. Loosen side of cake with knife or long, metal spatula; remove from pan.

In 1½-quart saucepan, melt butter over low heat; remove from heat. Stir in powdered sugar and lemon zest until smooth. Stir in lemon juice, 1 tablespoon at a time, until smooth and consistency of thick syrup. Spread glaze over top of cake, allowing some to drizzle down side.

Back to the State Fair

It was so much fun going to the Minnesota State Fair that I was determined to do it again. My State Fair pals became a group of like-minded friends, so we conspired to win trips again. It took a little more planning, as we didn't want to compete against each other. I decided to enter the dairy foods competition the next year and my friends selected other projects. We all made it to the fair again. My cheese soufflé demonstration won a blue ribbon and the Minnesota grand championship in dairy foods. Learning how to make that soufflé required a lot of studying, which seemed to me at the time less like cooking and more like a combination of physics and chemistry.

The next year I was again contemplating what to demonstrate in the 4-H competition. I'd done food preparation and dairy foods the previous two years. Now what?

One day Isä told me that he had eaten enough soufflés, omelets, and fluffy cakes. He announced that I should make some "real food."

"Hmm," I replied. "What would that be?"

"Rye bread!"

So the following year, I planned a demonstration making Finnish rye bread. First I had to scale down my mother's recipe. She would bake eighteen loaves of rye bread per batch—sometimes twice a week, even in the hot summertime.

I loved this bread and can recall its aroma wafting a quarter of a mile to the corner where the big yellow school bus dropped us off every day. We would run the length of the driveway, dump our books by the door, and head straight for the kitchen. When Mummy ordered us not to eat our fill of bread, and said that supper would be ready soon, we'd make a hole in the back of a loaf anyway and pull out soft warm bread. Betty Mae urged us on, saying, "Let's hurry up and eat it before we get full!"

In preparation for my rye bread demonstration I studied up on yeast, ideal dough temperatures, the relative gluten content in various kinds of flours, and the history of bread baking. I made loaf after loaf of Finnish rye bread and my father was quite happy.

Cooking Pays Off

★ ★ ★ ★ ★

4-H Champ Offered Date by Rotarians

BY CLARENCE ANDERSON
News-Tribune Staff Writer

A 16-year-old Floodwood 4-H club girl demonstrated her state championship cheese souffle to Duluth Rotarians yesterday and got herself:

About 180 unexpected guests for dinner.

An offer to meet a "nice, neat bachelor."

Beatrice Luoma, purple ribbon winner at the state fair this year, put on her apron and showed the Rotarians and fellow 4-H club achievement winners the step-by-step technique that won the purple.

Here's her recipe:

4 tablespoons butter
4 tablespoons flour
1 teaspoon salt
Dash of pepper
1½ cups of milk
½ pound of cheese
6 eggs

Make a white sauce of the butter, flour, flavoring and milk, then add the grated cheese, then beaten egg yolks. Fold this preparation into stiffly beaten egg whites and bake for an hour and one-quarter at 300 degrees.

The baking time worried the Rotarians, until she pulled out a golden, fluffy souffle she had previously mixed and baked. "Any questions?" she asked, proudly displaying the delicacy.

"Yes, when do we eat?" asked Rotarian Rudy Zweifel.

"I know a nice, neat bachelor you ought to meet," offered Dr. E. L. Tuohy.

The demonstration was part of 4-H achievement day, an annual club event. The club, through D. T. Grussendorf, south St. Louis county agriculture agent, and Robert Horton, 4-H club agent, gave achievement awards to:

Susan and Robert Riley, Floodwood; Ruth Ann Sramek, Meadowlands; Dennis Lindgren, Toivola; Keith Olson, Little Cloquet; Arnold Esterberg, Toivola; Betty Wagner, Adolph; Shirley Anderson, Hermantown, and Miss Luoma.

BEATRICE LUOMA
Gets 180 Dinner Guests

Winning the state championship through 4-H introduced me to a wider world of opportunities. This article ran in the Duluth News-Tribune *shortly after I won the blue ribbon.*

Cheese Soufflé

Sometimes I'd substitute a combination of other cheeses with success in this souf-flé. Today the cheese selection is a combination or a singular amount of Gruyère, Swiss, or flavored jack cheese that works well in place of the sharp cheddar. The soufflé can be totally assembled up to 2 hours before baking, but after baking you should be ready to serve it immediately because once it hits cool air it likes to sink.

Butter for coating the soufflé dish
2 tablespoons fine dry bread crumbs
¼ cup (½ stick) butter
¼ cup all-purpose flour
1¼ cups milk, heated

¼ teaspoon cayenne
¼ teaspoon salt
2 cups shredded sharp cheddar cheese
6 large eggs, separated
¼ teaspoon cream of tartar

Preheat the oven to 375°F. Generously butter a 2-quart soufflé dish and dust with the bread crumbs. Shake out any extra crumbs.

In a 3-quart pan over medium heat, melt the butter. Add flour and stir until mixture is smooth. Stir in the milk, cayenne, and salt, and continue to whisk until sauce boils and thickens, 3 to 4 minutes. Remove from heat.

Stir in the cheese until blended. Add the egg yolks and stir until the mixture is smooth. Set aside until cooled, but not cold.

In a clean, dry bowl, with a mixer on high speed, beat egg whites (use whisk attachment if available) with cream of tartar until short, stiff, moist peaks form and the bowl can be held upside down without the whites falling out.

With a flexible spatula, fold a third of the cheese sauce into whites until well blended. Add remaining sauce and gently fold in just until blended.

Scrape the batter into the prepared soufflé dish (or dishes). If the dish is more than ¾ full, make a foil collar* and fit it around the top of the dish. Draw a circle on the surface of the soufflé batter with the tip of a knife, about 1 inch in from rim, to help an attractive crown form during baking.

Bake for 25 to 30 minutes, until top is golden to deep brown and cracks look fairly dry. Serve immediately, scooping portions from single soufflé with a large spoon.

Makes 6 servings

---

* To make a foil collar, cut a 15-inch-wide sheet of foil 4 inches longer than circumference of dish; fold lengthwise in thirds. Brush one side of the foil strip generously with melted butter. Wrap the foil around outside of dish so that at least 2 inches of foil extend above the rim. Fold the ends of the buttered foil strip over several times until snug against dish.

As in past years, I again went through the process of practicing and practicing, kneading bread dough in my mind while working in the hay field, milking cows, and doing regular household chores. I explained the process of making bread to the trees, to the animals, to anything that I thought would listen. The words were so ingrained in my psyche that I could "motor mouth" to anybody about Finnish rye bread.

My rye bread demonstration won not only a trip to the State Fair but also a national grand championship and a trip to the national 4-H congress in Chicago! It was my first time traveling out of state.

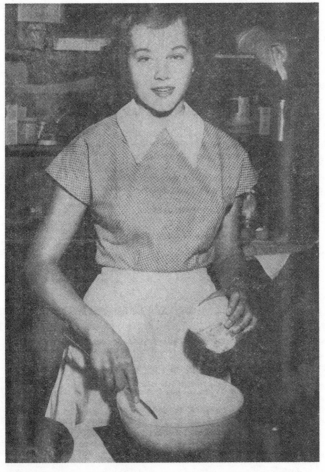

Demonstrating my state championship rye bread for an article in the Duluth News-Tribune *on November 4, 1951.*

Finnish Rye Bread

This is the bread most often made by Finns in Minnesota. Although my mother made a dozen and a half loaves at a time, I've worked the amounts down so that the recipe makes only one loaf. I've since also succumbed to quicker methods of mixing, so the directions include making the dough in the food processor as well as the bread machine with no reduction in the quality of the final product.

1 package (or 1 tablespoon) active dry yeast
½ cup warm water
1 cup additional water or warm potato water
1 tablespoon brown sugar
1 to 1½ cups stone-ground rye flour
1 tablespoon soft butter
1½ teaspoons salt
2 cups bread flour

Dissolve the yeast in the warm water. Combine water or potato water, brown sugar, and 1 cup rye flour to a large mixing bowl. Add yeast mixture and beat well. Stir in butter, salt, and most of the bread flour. Mix until a stiff dough forms. Sprinkle board with remaining ½ cup rye flour and turn dough out onto it. Cover with bowl and let rest for 10 minutes.

Knead the dough by folding it over onto itself over and over again until it is spongy and smooth, using rye flour to ease stickiness. You might not use all of the rye flour. Turn into a lightly oiled bowl, cover, and let rise until doubled. Punch down. Shape into a flat round loaf with a hole in the center, or shape into a plain round loaf. Let rise for 1 hour or until doubled. Prick all over with a fork. Bake at 375°F. for 45 to 50 minutes. Brush the loaf with butter while still hot.

Makes 1 loaf

To mix dough in food processor, measure all of the dry ingredients (use 1 cup rye flour) into the work bowl of the food processor. Turn motor on and slowly add 1¼ cups water or potato water through the feed tube; process until dough comes together and spins around the bowl, cleaning the bowl. Let rise, shape, and bake as directed above.

To mix dough in bread machine, measure all of the ingredients (use 1 cup rye flour) into the work bowl of the machine. Set machine to make "dough." Check during the mixing cycle; if necessary, add the remaining ½ cup rye flour. Shape, let rise, and bake as directed above.

Part II

Becoming a Home Economist

Nobody ever told me in so many words that my stories were or were not important. Perhaps by default, I have always felt that they were not. Yet ever since I was a young girl, even feeling this way, I have wanted to write. I've wanted to tell my stories. There seemed to be something magical about a blank piece of paper. I remember as a child being sick and confined to bed. The very best medicine anyone could give me then was a pad of paper and a pencil. I wrote poems and short stories, but I never dared let anybody see them.

Buried in boxes in the cluttered attic of our garage is a cloth-covered folder of my stories labeled "the works of Beatrice A. Luoma, age 15" that I had long ago laid to rest. I haven't opened the folder since, even though it was moved from one home to another in boxes of things that I didn't know what to do with. I don't even know why I saved it, but I just could not throw it away. In the box are stacks of rejection slips from *Calling All Girls* and *Seventeen* magazine clipped to the stories I had submitted hopefully and that routinely came back to me without so much as a handwritten signature. When I went to retrieve them from the upstairs of the garage, I found that the squirrels had made nests in the boxes and chewed all my precious papers to shreds.

Little glimmers of hope: essays and stories written as requirements of passage from one high school English class to another, pieces that usually came back marked with an A or an A minus. I assumed that was because most of my classmates hated to write and probably didn't do the assignments.

It was a young high school English teacher who, along with Tom Jacobson, the band director, and Tom Riley, the science teacher, convinced me that I really needed to go to college. It wasn't the usual thing a kid from Floodwood did at the time. Somehow, they found a hundred-dollar scholarship for me that was renewable for each of my four years of college. The money covered each year's tuition and student fees. In addition, I landed three part-time jobs at the university that covered my room and board, and I even earned enough money to send some home. Dorothy, the valedictorian of my class in Floodwood, who seemingly had no other ambition than to get married to her boyfriend and have babies, was offered full-ride scholarships to a number of colleges. I in turn had been offered a good-paying job at the Floodwood First State Bank, which I rejected. Counting money has never been my thing.

I ended up in the home economics department of the University of Minnesota Duluth, thinking I could squeeze in some of the creative writing classes that I lusted for. But home economics at that time was a terribly time-consuming course, with long labs where we learned skills like hat blocking and tailoring. The cooking labs were silly courses in which we boiled onions for two hours and then had to figure out why they were tasteless. I almost flunked the personal grooming class because I refused to wear a girdle.

Dr. Ruth was the head of the home economics department, and any deviation in my course of study had to be approved by her. I asked to take a creative writing course, which meant I had to drop one of the home economics requirements. I didn't mind tailoring and hat making, which were fun crafty classes and I really liked the teacher, but the education courses tested my endurance for pure monotony. I thought I could easily give up one of them.

Cooking in the home economics kitchen lab at the University of Minnesota Duluth in 1956.

Dr. Ruth called me into her office, where she presided behind her desk. A few papers neatly stacked to her left, my petition in front of her, a few well-sharpened pencils sticking out of a pottery mug on her right. Behind her was an original painting—an abstract. She liked to appear a patron of the arts. She was also in the middle of an affair with the head of the industrial arts department whose family lived just outside of town. I don't suppose his wife knew anything about it.

"Good morning, Be-atrice" (she always pronounced my name Be-atrice, although everybody else called me Peaches). She tipped her forehead forward, her eyes thin slits, as she stretched her thin lips across her nicotine-stained teeth. There was a space wide enough between her two front teeth to hold a cigarette.

She had dark, wavy hair that she pulled back into a bun and the lapel of her expensively tailored suit held a lovely designer silver sculpture.

Dr. Ruth grew up in Buffalo and I thought she acted like one. Her PhD was from Cornell University in Ithaca, New York, which I associated with bugs (the Finnish word for "insect" is *itikka*).

It did not take long to see that my wish was not going to be granted if I wanted to graduate on schedule. It did not take long, either, to realize that her disappointment in me was about the same as a farmer's when a cow doesn't produce. She counted the graduates as prizes, as she probably had promised me to fill one of the positions posted for home economics teachers.

"You have an obligation," she began, "to pay back your debt to society." She knew that I was engaged to be married shortly after my graduation. My fiancé, Dick, had been in ROTC and was stationed in England. Our plan was that he would fly home to attend the graduation, we'd get married, and then we would live in Oxford for a full year. She did not like that at all.

According to her, I was a leech on society. She told me that I would never grow up and that I would never need anything as frivolous as creative writing. I would have wasted my education.

There was no use arguing. The personal attacks I could handle, but what followed, I couldn't: "You come from the kind of family that doesn't know how to fold their sheets right." Anybody else might have laughed, but one thing that Finnish mothers teach their daughters is how to properly fold their linens. I left in tears.

Dr. Ruth died several years later, reportedly the only person ever allowed to smoke in the Benedictine Health Center.

A Turn in the Road

We met at the University of Minnesota Duluth at the beginning of my freshman year in 1952 as I set out to exert my independence from home, from home's everlasting responsibility on the farm. I loved the sweet taste of freedom for that brief period of time. I really didn't want to be tied down to anybody, no matter how nice. I wanted a career—as a writer, perhaps for a newspaper or magazine.

During my first month at the university my roommate, Wilma, and I were asked to help with mailing the *Statesman,* the university newspaper. We went to Washburn Hall, where we were to meet the staff. My job was to lick the stamps that were placed on the folded newspaper for mailing.

Wilma—or Willie, as she now likes to be called—was impressed by the "cute guys." I guess I didn't notice.

A few days later I got a phone call at Torrance Hall. "Hi! This is Dick Ojakangas!" a confident voice declared.

"Dick who?" I was puzzled.

Willie informed me quickly that Dick was that cute guy we met in Washburn Hall licking stamps for the *Statesman.* I really didn't remember.

I had been going home from school every second weekend, taking the Greyhound bus back to Floodwood. Dick drove home to the nearby town of Warba on weekends also, but on opposite weekends. After that day working on the *Statesman,* Dick persistently began asking me if I'd like to go to a movie "next weekend," or if I'd like a ride home. I persistently declared that I was not going home *that* weekend, or, that I was. I had a schedule, and I was keeping to it!

Later that quarter, there was a university event called the Engineers' Marriage Ball. Dick called and invited me to the ball. I told him that was my weekend to go home.

He asked me again and again, and again I insisted that I was going home that weekend. Finally, a mutual friend named Jack Hautaluoma (a roommate of Dick's and a fellow Floodwood graduate and longtime friend) sat me down with a cup of coffee in the cafeteria and asked me if I was going to the Marriage Ball. I told him that Dick had asked me several times but that I was going home that weekend.

At the Air Force ROTC dance at the University of Minnesota Duluth. Dick is in his ROTC
uniform next to Darlene Rosebaka. I was the runner-up (I didn't sell as many tickets).

"Aw, Peach!" he declared. "That's the big event of fall quarter! Everybody
goes to the Marriage Ball! You gotta tell Dick you will go!" I reluctantly agreed
that if he were to call again, I would accept the invitation.

Jack went back to the house where he and Dick rented rooms. He convinced Dick that I would, indeed, accept an invitation to the dance, even
though Dick had given up. Jack slapped a dollar bill down on the table and
said, "If she says no—that dollar is yours!"

Later, Dick called me. "Peach, would you like to go to the Marriage Ball
with me?"

"Oh, I'd love to go!" was my answer—even though I secretly thought the
idea was rather sinister.

It was by then the week of the ball, and I had to figure out what to wear. I
called home and had my parents send me the dress I had worn for homecoming the year before. They sent the dress down on the Greyhound bus, which
made its trip from Floodwood to Duluth every day.

The dance itself was frightening to me. A long line of suited male students paired with formally dressed female students took their turns ahead of us. In the lineup was an old chemistry professor and his wife. They simply walked around the big wedding ring on the platform, and I secretly thought, "There's my out!" We were supposed to step up to the betrothal-theme-decorated platform and, under the ring, kiss our partners.

We had never kissed before, and I was petrified! Dick tells me he really was eager to go through the ritual himself. So for a minute, I thought I could just walk around the platform like the chemistry professor and his wife. But then I stiffened and forced myself to go through with it.

That is all ancient history now.

It turned out that my ambition to write was a road covered with not rocks but boulders. (Dick, a geology graduate, jokingly told me he would put me into rocks as big as diamonds.) I ended up on the rigid path of home economics at the university because it seemed logical to me at the time. I didn't want to come to the university and just get my Mrs. degree. I truly wanted a degree that expanded my horizons. After all, if I were a writer, I reasoned with myself, I really needed to have something to write about and would have to expand my knowledge in a particular area. Home economics seemed like a broad field, one that covered not just food but family life, home design, aesthetics, and relationships. It seemed a continuation of my growing up, a life that was domestic rather than eclectic, being raised as the oldest of ten on a farm near a very rural community. What I knew best and understood best was the business of a household, and I was looking to expand that perspective and perhaps even write about it.

Alas, my selected major in home economics ended up being "nothing new" to me for the most part, and I found that the support studies (such as chemistry and physics) were much more interesting. The related arts of communications were deemed to be too esoteric to be in my curriculum, so I was denied entry into such studies by the head of the home economics department. I was supposed to follow through with education courses and become a teacher. My road to freedom was again, momentarily, blocked.

My First Taste of Gourmet Food

The first real "gourmet" food I tasted was food I cooked myself. In this case, it wasn't my own expertise—it was the quality of the ingredients and the inspiration in the form of menus and recipes from my employer that made the difference.

It was the end of my freshman year at the university, and a notice was posted on the home economics bulletin board. "Cook wanted for summer months, private home, must be a good cook." The pay? Room and board plus two hundred dollars per month. I applied, and my friend Marilyn applied for a housekeeper position there also. We both landed the summer jobs.

Mrs. Whitney was a widow with two sons, one enrolled at Stanford, the other working in the family business. She had duplicate copies of two-volume gold-embossed maroon *Gourmet Cookbooks,* as well as *Larousse Gastronomique,* Louis P. De Gouy's *The Gold Cook Book,* and other expensive volumes. One set of the books occupied her bedside table; the other, the bookshelf in the breakfast nook, where I could read and use them.

Mrs. Whitney would write out her menus for entertaining as a sort of bedtime reading. The next day she would present them to me as we discussed the day's plans. If she asked me to prepare something I had never heard of, I didn't let on. I would first look up key words in the dictionary, then in *Larousse,* and then check the indexes of the other cookbooks on the shelves. I usually found the right ingredients in her well-stocked kitchen. Sometimes I had to call Crystal's, a specialty food store in downtown Duluth, to have an unusual ingredient delivered.

Simpler menus—of which there were not many—were for when it was just Mrs. Whitney and her boys. But usually there was a party scheduled at the Whitney house. It followed a pattern. The drinks and appetizers were served in the "boathouse" by the lake. It was a grand building with floor-to-ceiling picture windows on the lakeside. The floor was covered with a lovely linen carpet from the now-defunct Klearflax Company in Duluth. Mrs. Whitney herself artistically designed the rug in shades of muted tans and blues so as to blend with the view of the lakeshore and the lake. The furniture and serving dishes were part of the total color scheme and picked up the sandy tan of the beach and the variegated blues of Sunshine Lake, which was visible through the windows.

The inevitable appetizer always included "lovely little vegetables"—tiny carrots, string beans, asparagus, radishes, and whatever else Mrs. Whitney with her prolific green thumb was able to grow in her vegetable garden and greenhouse. I arranged the tender little veggies in a huge cut glass bowl filled with shaved ice. Then I made an herbed cream dip with a hint of horseradish to accompany them.

It was fun making the hot appetizers, ranging from little cream puffs filled with pâté, deviled ham, cheese, fish, or meat mixtures to lobster, crab, chicken, or shrimp salad. The recipes were from the appetizer books of Helen Evans Brown. Sometimes they took the form of stuffing for the puffs, tiny tart shells, or itty-bitty cocktail quiches, all of which I made from scratch. We served smoked oysters on ice paired with hot, crispy pork sausages and cheesy-stuffed croutons served warm from the oven. There was also the ever-present appetizer of the day—"cheese puffs." Of course, the number of appetizers depended on the number of guests involved, which was usually ten

Hot Cheese Puffs

This appetizer was all the rage in the 1950s, and I made dozens of them over the course of the summer. They're easy to make ahead and bake at the last minute. They can also be made ahead and frozen.

4 ounces (half of an 8-ounce package) cream cheese, at room temperature
1 teaspoon grated fresh onion
½ cup mayonnaise (I usually made it fresh)
1 tablespoon chopped chives
Good dash of cayenne pepper
2 tablespoons grated Parmesan cheese
About 12 slices good-quality white bread

Preheat the oven to 350°F. In a medium bowl, mix the cream cheese with the onion, mayonnaise, chives, pepper, and Parmesan until well blended. Cut the bread into 1½-inch circles and spread each generously with the cheese mixture. Arrange on a baking sheet and bake for 15 minutes or longer for a crispier puff. Serve hot.

Makes about 12 servings

or twelve. Guests typically made their own cocktails from the well-stocked bar—thankfully, seeing as I really didn't know anything about mixing drinks. The guest list included regents of the University of Minnesota, local legislators, and other famous businesspeople from the area. This did not intimidate me. I simply followed directions specific to the menu.

After about an hour of cocktails and snacks, the guests entered the dining room. I never got to see them because Marilyn was the waitress and was appropriately dressed with a white frilly apron over a black skirt and blouse.

Burnt Sugar Ice Cream

A favorite of the house was this simple, delicious ice cream that was smooth and creamy, flavored with burned sugar. It was a staple in the freezer and we could indulge ourselves whenever we wished. This is a simple-to-make ice cream that can be frozen in a refrigerator tray or in a hand freezer. The secret to the texture of this ice cream is to chill the evaporated milk until icy, and use a hand mixer to whip until fluffy. The basic recipe came from De Gouy's *The Gold Cook Book*.

⅓ cup granulated sugar
1 cup milk, scalded
⅛ teaspoon salt
2 egg yolks, slightly beaten
1 teaspoon pure vanilla extract
1½ cups (or 1 can) undiluted evaporated milk, chilled and whipped

Sprinkle the sugar into a heavy skillet and place over medium heat, stirring often until the sugar dissolves and turns a caramel brown.

When sugar is browned, stir in the hot milk. Stir until sugar crystals are completely dissolved, or for about 5 minutes.

In a heatproof bowl, combine the salt and egg yolks. Add 2 tablespoons of the hot mixture to temper them, being careful not to actually scramble the yolks.

Slowly whisk the caramel milk into the egg mixture, mixing constantly. Pour the custard into the skillet. Cook until the mixture coats a spoon, stirring constantly. Remove from the heat and chill.

Fold in the whipped milk and pour the creamy mixture into a freezer tray or hand freezer and freeze until mushy. Remove from the refrigerator tray and beat until very smooth. Return to the freezer and freeze about three hours until firm.

Makes about 1½ pints of ice cream or 6 servings

Usually there would be a first course. It was sometimes mushrooms with garlic butter or oysters with caviar or some other "little" dish. This would be followed by soup and croutons or crisp homemade crackers. Then we served a filet of beef or coq au vin or canard à l'orange, or some other "lovely" main course, and a special vegetable, delicate green salad, or Mrs. Whitney's favorite molded black cherry salad flavored heavily with port wine and a freshly baked small bread. Dessert was often homemade cookies and burnt sugar ice cream. Every dish, every course, was a learning experience for me. Food, for the first time in my life, took on especially delicate flavors.

Between courses, Mrs. Whitney would buzz us in from the kitchen using a button on the floor under the table. Since she had usually imbibed considerable amounts by then, she often had trouble finding the button. I never saw this, but Marilyn would report the progress of her inebriation.

Afterward, Mrs. Whitney would always report her delight regarding the meal to Marilyn and give her all the praise. I seemed to be nonexistent—except for the fact that I had done all the cooking and baking. But then again, I was happy to "hide" in the kitchen. The most valuable lesson I learned from that summer in the kitchen on the beautiful shore of Sunshine Lake was how food—well prepared with high-quality ingredients—should taste.

My "Toast in the Morning Man"

By the end of my time at the university, Dick and I were engaged to be married. For our wedding date, we chose Sunday, June 10, 1956, after I graduated on Friday with my B.S. degree in home economics. I really wanted to graduate with my maiden name of Luoma. I was the first person in our family to go to college and earn a degree. Dick had spent the year in England at Upper Heyford near Oxford as a second lieutenant. He rented an apartment and bought a little tan Volkswagen.

Meanwhile, I was nearing graduation, having recently completed a stint in the "Home Management House" that was part of the requirements. I hadn't been allowed to test out of it—no one was, regardless of experience—even though I had spent a year working for my room and board at a home as a cook and household assistant to an elderly couple who lived near the campus. Plus, as the oldest of ten kids at home, I was already well versed in planning meals, cleaning the house, balancing a budget, and handling the usual tasks of running a household. Yet for all that, I still had to complete the course.

The Home Management House was situated in a large brick mansion that had been donated to the university by a wealthy family. It had beautiful sweeping staircases, several fireplaces, and spacious rooms. The large kitchen had a butler's pantry, and the dining room was formal. There were six students in each session, and we all had our private bedrooms, as did the teacher—who was no other than Dr. Ruth. When she was not in the house, we goofed around, posing at the mantel, sliding down the staircase, and dancing on the dining room table.

The most exciting thing about the house, though, was that we had to take turns planning meals. Breakfast, especially, was total fun. "Esoteric" breakfast breads like scones and muffins were something we rarely made at home except on a Sunday afternoon—when, of course, it wasn't breakfast time, but good for afternoon coffee, especially if company were coming. The table at Home Management House was always formally set—for all three meals!

While at the house, I surreptitiously sewed my wedding dress and the formals for all of my wedding attendants—my sisters. I had found a wedding dress at Oreck's Bridal Shop in downtown Duluth and went back to the shop multiple times to "try" it on. Each time, I took more notes on the design and

Our wedding day, June 10, 1956. I made my own dress on the sly in Home Management class, as well as three bridesmaid dresses for my sisters.

the fabric that made up the dress. It was white satin with a fitted bodice, fitted long sleeves, and thirty-six covered buttons marching up the back.

In my spare time, I made a pattern for the dress and then a mock garment of muslin. In the final rendition, I covered the little round buttons with satin and made the satin loop fasteners. I did all this without Dr. Ruth knowing anything about it. Of course, my fellow classmates knew all along and encouraged me.

I graduated on a Friday evening in Duluth, and Dick and I were married two days later in Floodwood. The church was filled with the aroma of buckets of lilacs that we cut from the bushes around the house on our farm. We packed the sanctuary with family and UMD friends. It was about ninety degrees and just as humid.

The reception afterward was held in the basement of the church. The ladies had prepared sandwiches, bars, and cookies, and they served Kool-Aid and coffee.

The following Thursday we flew to Oxford, England, where Dick had rented an apartment up from City Centre on Banbury Road. This was after a brief sort of "honeymoon" trip—basically just to get away from relatives—

into western Wisconsin, where Dick, ever the enthusiastic geologist, wanted to show me tiny stalactites in a minuscule cave. I've never forgotten that first geology lesson: stalactites drop from the ceiling of the cave while stalagmites grow up from the floor of the cave.

Our apartment in Oxford had an eighteen-inch electric stove in the kitchen with solid metal burners that took forever to heat up. The oven was narrow but just wide enough for a twelve-inch cookie sheet. The kitchen was the size of an average closet.

Even in my limited space, I enjoyed preparing meals—especially breakfast. I applied the skills I learned at university to my newly minted life, and that was great fun. I planned to make scones of different flavors, muffins in all possible varieties, biscuits, and fruit and nut pancakes for breakfast every morning.

I shopped in the nearby greengrocer's, the dairy, and the fishmonger. Mostly I enjoyed shopping in the outdoor market on weekends. I would ride the red double-decker bus to Banbury on Saturday mornings. It didn't take long to learn that merchants never offered bags in which to put your purchases—people brought their own shopping bags and baskets. One day, I found beautiful brussels sprouts and bought a pound of them. Dismayed that I had nothing to put them in, I found a solid antique copper kettle in the next stall, at what I thought was a bargain price. It had a lid and a sturdy han-

dle, so I filled it with the sprouts. That kettle sits next to our wood-burning stove today in our living room, a prized possession.

Over the door of our apartment on Banbury Road was an attractive, heavy, brass-and-copper plate with Cyrillic script all over it. We thought it was artistic, but later found that it had been left there by Iraqi students who lived in the apartment before us. We traded several small items we knew we wouldn't need anymore, like electrical adapters and plugs, to the landlords for that piece. The plate still hangs in our house today.

In England, circa 1956.

Dick would invite local English geologists, all students at Oxford, for dinner—and I truly enjoyed cooking for them. The meals were simple: I used recipes from a Betty Crocker Junior cookbook, baked yeast bread, and for dessert usually made American-style apple pies.

After a couple of weeks of my "creative" breakfast breads, almond scones, fruit-filled muffins, flaky biscuits, and the like, Dick broke his news to me: "I'm a toast in the morning man!" That ended my first foray into creative quick breads.

Almond Cardamom Scones

I often whip up these scones, perfumed with cardamom and crunchy with almonds, to serve a large group of people for a breakfast meeting or an afternoon gathering. They go well with hot spiced cider or spiced tea.

3 cups all-purpose flour
1 tablespoon baking powder
1 teaspoon freshly ground cardamom
½ cup sugar
1 cup chopped almonds
1 cup (2 sticks) unsalted butter, frozen
3 large eggs
½ to ⅔ cup plain yogurt or buttermilk
1 tablespoon sugar

Preheat the oven to 400°F. Lightly grease a large cookie sheet or cover with parchment paper.

Combine flour, baking powder, cardamom, sugar, and almonds in a large bowl. Grate the frozen butter onto the flour mixture.

Mix the eggs and ½ cup of the yogurt or buttermilk in a small bowl. Add to the dry ingredients and blend quickly, just until a dough forms. (Add a bit more yogurt or buttermilk if needed.)

Using an ice-cream scoop, place mounds of dough on the cookie sheet, about 3 inches apart. Sprinkle tops with the sugar.

Bake 8 to 10 minutes until light brown. Cool on a wire rack. Serve warm.

Makes 24 scones

The Pillsbury Bake-Off

Our flat on Banbury Road in Oxford was about fifteen miles away from the air force base in Upper Heyford where Dick was stationed. Oxford is only about sixty miles from London, so we often took in operas, stage plays, and concerts during the time we lived there. We enjoyed Verdi's *Rigoletto* and *La Traviata*, and Puccini's *La Bohème*, among other famous operas.

We drove to London in our little tan Beetle, which Dick had purchased for $950 through the base exchange (the PX). The Beetle was built for the British market, with the driver's seat on the right side, and we drove on the left side of the road. It petrified me to think of driving on the narrow roads that wound through the countryside, skirting farms, pubs, and little settlements.

One night in the fall of 1956, heading home after a particularly long opera, Dick was having trouble staying awake and I was no help with the driving.

"Peach, talk to me! Keep me awake! Talk about anything, but just start talking!"

So I did. I remembered a few days before that, at the Officers' Wives Club, the base commander's wife had held up entry blanks to the Pillsbury Bake-Off. Waving the forms around, she announced, "If you want to win a bunch of money—here are the entry blanks—I'll put them in the women's john!" I had forgotten to take one, but was thinking I should enter something.

"What should I enter?" I asked Dick.

"Why not that good bread you've been baking?"

"Well," I said, "I've got to do something different with it."

We discussed the possibilities for a while. I had been lonesome for the kind of dark bread that I loved at home, and the best I could do in England was to make a bread using molasses for darkening, and cornmeal, an ingredient I found in the local market under the name of "maize." I cooked the cornmeal, darkened it with molasses, and made it into a yeast-raised round loaf.

"What if I made the bread into a great big cheese sandwich?" I wondered. "It could have a layer of cheese through the middle, and we could cut it into wedges like pie—wouldn't that be great for a picnic?"

We discussed that possibility and agreed that I should make the bread the very next day. Dick agreed to pick up an entry blank the next day, too. (I don't know how he broke into the women's john.)

Looking at the entry form, we found to our surprise that the postmark deadline was the next day. I would have to hurry.

The cupboard had just enough ingredients to make the bread once. Expecting a beautiful round loaf with a layer of cheese when I opened the oven door, I found instead that the cheese had melted and oozed out, covering the rack and the bottom of the oven. Disappointment!

As I picked the loaf apart, I discovered a few remnants of the cheese suspended in the golden brown crumbs of the bread. It tasted great!

What to do? I wrote down the recipe, but instead of a thick layer of cheese through the middle of the loaf, I thought it just might work if I cut the cheese into cubes and kneaded them into the dough as I shaped it. But I didn't have enough ingredients or time to try that option, so I just wrote down the recipe, filled out the entry blank, and got the untested recipe into the base mail just in time to be postmarked by the deadline.

Fast-forward nine months.

Dick was finished with his air force duty and we were temporarily staying in his parents' home in Warba, Minnesota. It was 1957, and he had accepted a temporary one-year position at our alma mater, the University of Minnesota Duluth, while they searched for another addition to the department. We were waiting to get into a rented apartment near the campus. I was pregnant with our first child.

The phone in Warba rang. The call was for me.

"Congratulations! You are one of the one hundred finalists in the Pillsbury Bake-Off!" the voice said.

With "movie star" Ronald Reagan at the Pillsbury Bake-Off in Beverly Hills, October 1957.

I was stunned. "When is the Bake-Off?"

I was told it was being held on October 14 in Los Angeles—the very same day the baby was due. Besides that, my copy of the recipe was packed away in household goods that wouldn't arrive from England until December. Plus, I never really had made the bread according to the recipe I submitted. When a representative from Pillsbury came to Warba to have me sign the entry papers for the Bake-Off, I surreptitiously copied the recipe over his shoulder.

The news of my being a finalist in the contest hit the local newspapers. I didn't know what to do. My doctor thought I was crazy even to consider going to Los Angeles in my condition, but letters and phone calls from friends and relatives all encouraged me to *go!* I signed my letter saying I would go "conditions permitting."

Our daughter, Cathy, was conveniently born on October 1. About a week after I came home from the hospital, I flew to Los Angeles and stayed at the Beverly Hilton. My mother took care of the baby, who wasn't allowed to fly yet. All the exciting events planned for the one hundred finalists escaped me. I was like a sick cow—brimming with milk, desiring nothing but my new child. I wanted to nurse her like a real mother, but I spent every spare minute in the bathroom with a breast pump.

Our pediatrician back home, the kindly Finnish Dr. Leppo, had encouraged me: "You need to use a breast pump, and you can nurse the baby when you get home."

Later, someone asked my mother if she had fed the baby with a bottle while I was gone. Her answer, "That was the best I could do!"

Being awarded the Second Grand Prize at the Pillsbury Bake-Off came as a shock to me. Copyright 1957 Star Tribune.

At the Beverly Hilton, the excitement was palpable. I was among the hundred women, with recipes in hand, marching into the huge ballroom equipped with one hundred ranges and worktables. The tables were loaded with ingredients enough to make our recipes three times over. I baked my loaves and then they were whisked off to the judges.

We each had our photo taken with the then-host of *The General Electric Theater*, Ronald Reagan. He looked totally bored as he posed and faked a smile, pointing to something "out there." (This was before he became known as the "Great Communicator.")

I was excited for the awards banquet because I knew I would be going home the next day. To my utter surprise, Art Linkletter announced the winners. "The five-thousand-dollar Second Grand Prize goes to"— he lifted the dome off my loaf of bread—"Mrs. Richard Ojakangas!" I had won! Even if they hadn't called *my* name—in those days, women didn't have first names but were identified by whom they were married to. But I had won! The downside was that I had to stay in Los Angeles an extra day.

People often ask me what I did with the five thousand dollars. I did what women in that day did: it paid for two years of my husband's education as he went for his master's degree in geology at the University of Missouri in Columbia.

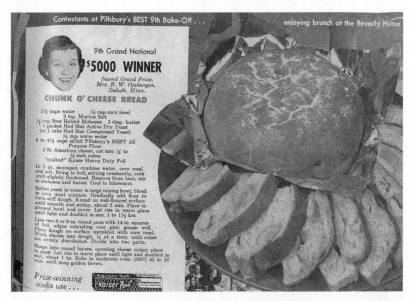

This advertisement featuring the recipe for Chunk o' Cheese Bread ran in Better Homes and Gardens.

Cheesy Picnic Bread (Chunk o' Cheese Bread)

When I entered this recipe in the Bake-Off competition, I used the name "Cheesy Picnic Bread." Pillsbury later changed the name to "Chunk o' Cheese Bread." Today I use a medium sharp cheddar cheese instead of the processed American cheese I used in the original recipe.

1¾ cups water
½ cup cornmeal
2 teaspoons salt
½ cup dark molasses
2 tablespoons butter
1 package or 1 tablespoon active dry yeast
½ cup warm water (105°F to 115°F)
4 to 5 cups bread flour
1 pound sharp cheddar cheese, cut into ½-inch cubes

In a medium saucepan, stir together water, cornmeal, and salt. Bring the mixture to a boil, stirring constantly, until thickened. Remove from heat and stir in the molasses and butter. Set aside to cool to room temperature.

In a large bowl, dissolve the yeast in the warm water. Let sit until creamy, about ten minutes. Add the cornmeal mixture and 2 cups of the flour; beat well. Add the remaining flour ½ cup at a time, mixing well after each addition. When the dough comes together, turn it out onto a lightly floured surface. Knead until smooth and elastic, about 10 minutes. (Today, I'd put it into my heavy-duty mixer with the dough hook in place, and mix for 10 minutes, scraping the sides of the bowl often.) Place the dough in a lightly oiled bowl and turn to coat with oil. Cover with a damp cloth and let rise in a warm place until doubled in volume, about 1 hour.

Turn dough out onto a lightly floured surface and flatten. Place ⅓ of the cheese cubes on the flattened dough and fold the dough up to enclose the cubes. Do this twice more, until all of the cheese is incorporated into the dough. You may have to let the dough rest for a few minutes between folding. Divide the dough into two equal pieces and form each piece into a round loaf.

Place the rounds on lightly greased baking sheets, cover with plastic wrap, and let rise until nearly doubled, about 45 minutes. Preheat the oven to 350°F.

Bake in the preheated oven for 45 to 55 minutes or until golden brown and the bottom of the loaf sounds hollow when tapped.

Makes 2 loaves, about 20 servings

A Year in Finland

A few years after the Pillsbury Bake-Off, in 1960–61, we spent a year in Finland because Dick had applied for and received a student Fulbright. The difference between a student Fulbright and a family grant was that the grant he received was just enough for one person (i.e., the student) to live on. Needless to say, our funds while we were in Finland that year were meager.

Others in the group had enough money to rent rather luxurious apartments in prestigious sections of Helsinki. We rented a one-bedroom apartment on the third floor of a building for retired nurses in a northern suburb called Käpylä. At the time, our daughter Cathy was almost three and our son, Greg, was a year old. Yet I felt privileged to be in the same country that my grandparents had left behind.

The Arctic Circle runs through Finland. When we first arrived in Helsinki, the days seemed the normal length, about the same as what we'd left in Minnesota. But as autumn faded into winter, they quickly became shorter and shorter, and soon it was dark by three in the afternoon. Being a person affected by solar deficiency, I didn't know what was coming over me. I had never experienced the kind of "sadness" that began to color my days.

To add to the stress, Dick spent every day, all day, at the Geological Survey and the university, leaving me to care for our two children, carrying them both up and down three flights of stairs (the building had no elevator). This was good exercise, but it became a challenge when I had to bring home milk and other groceries. To add to that, the nearest bus stop was six blocks away, so it was a major effort to go to downtown Helsinki. I was very limited in what I was able to do.

Finally, one day out of exasperation, I called the United States Information Service—the organization that had been involved in our orientation—and explained my dilemma. I said that I could speak Finnish and that I could present cooking demonstrations on American foods. I told them I'd be willing to travel, but would need my expenses covered. They jumped on the idea and scheduled me to visit women's organizations in villages throughout the country. I was to stay in the homes of my sponsors, and my travel expenses would be fully covered.

Wow! The only limitation was that I could travel only on weekends, when Dick's schedule made it possible for him to stay home with Cathy and Greg. The foods of America were exotic to Finns at the time. I had received boxes of cake mixes through my connections with Pillsbury. They were a revolutionary idea for Finnish cooks. I made popcorn and impressed them with the "before and after" volume. I cooked hamburgers and made apple pie.

The women I visited belonged to an organization called the Marttaliitto, or the Martha League, which was similar to women's organizations that in Minnesota were organized by the county agent. They all came into the schoolroom and placed their chairs in a circle. Each woman pulled out knitting or crocheting as she attentively listened to what I had to say. Always willing to share, the women scribbled their recipes on scraps of paper, the backs of envelopes, whatever paper they had on hand. Throughout my visits,

Lanttulaatikko (Rutabaga Casserole)

Cooked and mashed rutabaga, often mixed with mashed potatoes, can be made with either turnips or rutabagas. This dish is not only traditional, but a *must* for the holiday buffet. Home-cured ham is the usual meat for the holidays.

2 medium rutabagas, peeled and diced, about 6 cups or 3 cups rutabagas
    and 3 cups diced peeled potatoes
¼ cup dry bread crumbs
¼ cup heavy cream
½ teaspoon ground nutmeg
1 teaspoon salt
2 eggs, beaten
3 tablespoons butter

Preheat the oven to 350°F. Butter a 2½-quart casserole and set aside.
    Cook the rutabagas or rutabagas and potatoes together in salted water to cover until soft.
    Drain and mash. Soak the bread crumbs in the cream and stir in the nutmeg, salt, and beaten eggs.
    Blend mixture with the mashed rutabagas and potatoes. Turn into the casserole. Dot the top with butter. Bake for 1 hour or until the top is lightly browned.

Serves 6

Swedish Prince's (Princess) Cake

Greg had his first birthday on the Swedish ship the M.S. *Kungsholm* on our trip to Finland, and his second on the Norwegian ship *Stavangerfjord* when we returned to the United States. We packed everything we thought we would need for a year into two steamer trunks, four suitcases, and overnight bags—we hadn't yet learned to travel light. We boarded the *Kungsholm* on the way to Göteborg, Sweden, where we caught a train to Stockholm, and from there a ferry to Helsinki. The journey took lots of strength and energy! In Göteborg, we bought a double stroller to make walking with two little kids easier.

Greg's first birthday was August 14, while we were in the mid-Atlantic. The pastry chef baked him a "Prince's Cake"—a Swedish classic for such celebrations. If Greg had been female, it would have been called a "Princess Cake." They are exactly the same cake, except for girls the marzipan coating would be tinted pink. The cake is a triple-layered creation with fillings of raspberry jam, pastry cream, and whipped cream, blanketed by a layer of marzipan. It's not a cake you start making at 4:00 P.M. with plans to serve it by 7:00! I suggest that you make it in stages: first make the pastry cream, because it has to cool; then bake the cake. After it cools, slice it horizontally in three layers. You need to top it with a rounded mound of whipped cream to be authentic, so slip the cake into the freezer for a couple of hours so that it is easier to form the marzipan over the top. Don't let the daunting list of ingredients overwhelm you—each part of the cake is quite simple to prepare. In the end you have a beautiful cake!

Pastry cream

> 2 cups whole milk
> ½ cup sugar
> 4 egg yolks (save whites for cake)
> ⅓ cup cornstarch
> 1 teaspoon vanilla
> ¼ cup softened butter

Cake

> 2 cups sugar
> 2 eggs plus 4 egg whites
>   (at room temperature)
> 2 cups all-purpose flour
> 2 teaspoons baking powder
> 1 cup milk
> ½ cup (1 stick) butter
> 1 teaspoon vanilla extract

Simple syrup

> ¼ cup water
> 1 tablespoon rum if desired
> ¼ cup sugar

Filling and marzipan layer

> 2 cups heavy cream, whipped stiff,
>   slightly sweetened if desired
> ½ cup seedless raspberry jam
> 3 (7-ounce) packages marzipan
> Green and red food coloring
> Powdered sugar for dusting

For the pastry cream, heat the milk with half of the sugar to a simmer. Meanwhile, whisk the yolks, remaining sugar, and cornstarch. When the milk-and-sugar mixture is hot, whisk a little of it at a time into the yolk mixture. Cook until thickened, whisking constantly, about 2 minutes. The cream becomes very thick. Beat in the vanilla and butter. Cool completely.

For the cake, preheat the oven to 350°F. Grease and flour a 10-inch springform pan and line the bottom with a circle of parchment paper. Coat with nonstick spray.

Beat the sugar, eggs, and egg whites together until very light and thick; this takes 5 to 10 minutes at high speed, a task that is most easily done in an electric stand mixer. Stir the flour and baking powder together. Heat the milk, butter, and vanilla extract until the butter is melted and milk is steaming. Blend the flour mixture into the eggs and slowly add the hot milk and butter, whisking constantly until batter is smooth and thick. Pour the batter into the prepared pan and bake for 45 to 50 minutes until the cake bounces back when lightly touched in the center and a toothpick inserted into the center comes out clean and dry. Remove from the oven and cool completely on a rack. Remove cake from the pan.

For the simple syrup, cook the water and sugar until sugar is melted. Cool and add rum, if desired. Refrigerate any remaining syrup.

Using a long knife, cut the cake horizontally into three even layers. Place the bottom layer, cut side up, on a sheet of waxed paper. Brush with 2 tablespoons simple syrup and spread with about ½ cup of the whipped cream and with the raspberry jam, spreading to the edges of the layer.

Place what was the top of the cake, cut side up, on top of the whipped cream. Brush with 2 tablespoons simple syrup and spread to the edges with a very thin layer of whipped cream and then with all the cooled pastry cream. Top with the remaining layer of cake, brush with simple syrup, and pile the remaining whipped cream on top of the cake. (At this point you can refrigerate or freeze the cake to top with the marzipan blanket later.)

For the marzipan layer, soften the marzipan and reserve a golf ball–sized portion and set aside. Cut remaining mixture into pieces and knead about half with your hands until pliable, working in green food coloring. (This is most easily done in the food processor with the steel blade in place.) Roll out between sheets of plastic wrap to make a 16-inch circle. Dust with powdered sugar if desired. Transfer marzipan onto the cake by rolling it up on the rolling pin and then unrolling it over the cake. Smooth out with your hands, covering the cake completely; trim off excess marzipan. Color the uncolored golf ball–sized portion with red food coloring, roll it out into a strip, trim the edges, and roll up to resemble a rose. Place on the cake. You can refrigerate the cake up to 3 days before serving.

Makes about 12 servings

I kept asking about Finnish food traditions, about their customs during holidays, and what certain Finnish words meant. These were words my grandmother used, but I wasn't thinking enough when she was alive to ask what they meant. Words such as *rieska* and *laatikko*. People were ever so willing to give me their recipes; I made notes everywhere I went and collected wonderful information and recipes, all of which eventually provided fodder for my first book, *The Finnish Cookbook*.

Stories from Finland

During our year in Finland, I wrote a half dozen columns for my hometown newspaper, the *Floodwood Forum*, about our experiences while traveling. When cleaning out my parents' home some time ago, I found three of the articles packed away in a stash of papers. I had totally forgotten that I had written them.

What follows here are those three missives from Finland. The first scene takes place during the few days after Christmas while we were visiting relatives in Kauhajoki. Kerttu Risku was an English teacher in the village school and had a good command of the language. She volunteered to help me find and read the records in the Kurikka church. Finland, at the time, kept all the records of births and deaths in church archives. Here is the article as published in the *Floodwood Forum*.

In the last "News from Finland" I told you about our Christmas in Etelä Pohjanmaa with Lilja and Kerttu Risku. This is the part of Finland where most of Dick's and my grandparents came from. We took advantage of the time we had to check up on the family tree.

Kerttu and I went to Kurikka, which is about ten kilometers from Kauhajoki, where Dick's grandmother was born. My mother's mother was born in Kurikka. We didn't have much of a clue where to start from, when we first entered the modern building where the church records are kept.

We started with the records of 1880. There we found Amanda Aurora Tassi, born May 27, 1883. Her father, my great-grandfather, was Jaakko Tassi, and his lineage we traced back to 1700 (there were fires at that time that destroyed church records).

We visited the farm where Amanda Aurora was born. The people living there [in 1960] had the name of Aarne Rinta-Tassi and were my mother's cousins. It was a thrill to meet such lively, friendly people, and they were thrilled to meet "American relatives." There were many stories told about the Tassi family.

After that, we drove to Kokkola, where a cousin of my mother lived. Under her direction we found the town of Sievi, where an old aunt

was still living in an "old folks' hospital." I was impressed with the way
Finland cares for the elderly.
"Eliina Täti" was in a room with two other old ladies. One was
ninety-six years old—a Carelian, and still as spry as ever, but had a
broken hip bone. We took pictures of them and you'd have thought we
gave them a million dollars, they were so impressed.
The most exciting moment of this visit was when Eliina Tati looked
at me and said that somehow I looked like her sister, Ruusu (Amanda
Aurora). We found old photos of my grandmother and were amazed at
the resemblance between her and my mother.
I don't think anything can be more thrilling than to find out about
ancestors. We have looked into other branches of the family tree too,
but they are more difficult to locate.

I also wrote articles about my time traveling around Finland, courtesy of the
United States Information Service, to talk to Finnish women about American
food.

I've had the most interesting few days again, giving demonstrations at
Rovaniemi.
The most striking thing about Rovaniemi, which is in Lapin lääni,
the farthest north of Finland's cities, was the sparkling, absolutely
brilliant sunshine. I have never experienced such a beautiful winter
sun—not even in Minnesota!
One of the first things that came up in my conversation with the
teachers at the school I visited was the exact location of the Arctic
Circle. According to the map, Rovaniemi is exactly on the Arctic
Circle. But I was told that the Arctic Circle changes, according to the
occasion. The most prominent change (and the best-kept secret of the
time) was the time Eleanor Roosevelt visited Rovaniemi. It was a big
occasion for her to see the Arctic Circle. But she didn't know that until
that time, not much was made of the Arctic Circle except that people
knew it was there. It was "moved" to a convenient spot, and a special
hut was constructed and special markers made. There was some "last-
minute rush" I was told. The last nails were driven and fresh paint
was drying as Eleanor's plane landed.
The people who "made" the Arctic Circle had to rush and clean up
and then dress up in their Lapp costumes and greet the gal! I guess
Rovaniemi is much like the typical American town where there are a
few people who do everything.
The Finns and Lapps were much taken by Eleanor. They liked her.

In fact, last fall when Dick was in Rovaniemi, he met a Lapp who had proposed to her and if she wasn't married the next time she came to Rovaniemi he would marry her. At last report they were both still unattached. By the way, this fellow has a brother in Minnesota.

Well, the Arctic Circle was not moved for me (sigh). I did go to see the markers, though, and had my picture taken next to it. I demonstrated hamburgers, apple pie, lemon pie, and popcorn to the Rovaniemians. Again, popcorn stole the show.

I had had plans to visit a relative near Rovaniemi, my uncle Frank's wife's sister. But alas, I found that she lived about forty miles out of Rovaniemi, southward, toward Kemi. So, we must leave that visit until next summer.

One of the funniest things happened in Kajaani, the other city I visited. The director of the school had reserved a hotel room for me under the name "Ojakangas." Well, another Ojakangas walked in just before me and took the room! It was sheer coincidence as even in Finland our name is an odd one. The most pleasant thing was that for the first time, we met another Ojakangas. Are we related?

The hotel quickly got me another room with apologies!

In another article later that year, I wrote about our experiences with the wonderful Finnish tradition of Vappu.

Finland has burst into springtime!

It's May 5 and the grass has been green already for a couple of weeks, crocuses are blooming, pussy-willows are almost little leaves, and the kids have eliminated their heavy winter clothes. It all seemed to happen the weekend of May Day. In Finland it is called "Vappu" and is a very big celebration. It is like our homecomings and proms and Fourth of July all in one. People just go crazy. Downtown was as colorful as it ever is during the whole year. Mostly, it was due to the people selling balloons. The bunches of balloons are the biggest things I have ever seen; they are at least twice as tall as the people selling them. There were hundreds of balloon salesmen all over town—balloons of all colors. Every little kid had one. We ended up buying a new balloon every day, expensive as they were. The cheapest balloons sold for 100 marks (about 32 cents) and the price ranged all the way up to 1,000 marks! Besides balloons, colorful shakers, streamers, party masks and hats added to the scene.

Sunday night was "Vappu Eve"—always the night before May 1st and is the traditional University Student holiday. The order of the day is to stay up all night. We hadn't planned on doing much but looking around downtown, seeing "Haavis Amanda" (a statue of a woman in the center of a fountain) get crowned with a white University Student's cap, at midnight, and to see all of the students put on their white caps, too. Luckily, we have a friend who used to be a student and he got us into a couple of student dances, one before midnight and one after— for the sake of seeing student life in action.

All I can say is that UMD was never like this. The holiday spirit added to the atmosphere, but these dances were really wild. We couldn't help but think what our "chaperones" at dances really stop.

The next day we saw Finnish humor in action. May Day during the day is meant for the kids, so we took ours to the traditional spot "Ullanlinna" where the students have a program. There, an "ooompa German band," as we would call it, made up of university students was playing. It was a beautiful warm day and the band started from

May Day Tippaleipä

These fritters are served in Finland during the May Day celebrations along with a homemade sparkling beverage called Sima.

1 cup milk
2 eggs
½ teaspoon salt
2 cups all-purpose flour
Hot oil or fat for frying
Powdered sugar

Stir the milk, eggs, salt and flour until smooth.

Heat the fat or oil to 375°F. Pour about 1 cup of the batter into a small, heavy-duty plastic bag with a zip-top closure. With scissors, cut a tiny hole in one corner, about 1/8 inch in diameter. Drizzle the batter into the hot fat, swirling the bag in a continuous round to form a bird's nest shape, three or four inches in diameter.

Fry 1 minute on each side. Remove from fat and drain on paper towels. Sift powdered sugar over.

Makes about 15 tippaleipä

the top of a hill in a park, played a couple of pieces and the students would dance until they stumbled on a stone or on a stump, and laugh. This "rickety" band meandered all over town stopping here and there, sometimes climbing a tree or onto the top of a car and then they would play there.

Finns are usually reserved, but not on May Day. That is their one day to let off steam and be as goofy as they wish and do everything to excess. The next day they settle down to be their usual reserved selves.

There was a Communist parade somewhere in town. Nobody bothered to attend when it was in downtown Helsinki. A few marched around displaying medals and Russian flags.

Now, the next day, the town is quiet, the balloons are gone and the people are exhausted. But it was during this holiday that spring sprang!

Sima

This is a non-alcoholic, lemon-flavored fizzy drink.

4 quarts water
1 cup brown sugar
1 cup granulated sugar
2 lemons, washed and thinly sliced
1/8 teaspoon dry yeast
1 tablespoon raisins plus extra sugar

Heat the water to boiling and stir in the sugars. Add the lemon slices. Cool to lukewarm. Pour into a non-metal container such as an ice-cream pail. Add the yeast. Let stand at room temperature overnight or at least 8 to 10 hours until little bubbles appear around the edges of the liquid.

Strain the liquid into sterilized bottles (8 pints or 4 quarts). Add 1 teaspoon sugar and a few raisins to each bottle. Cork tightly. Let stand at room temperature until the raisins have risen to the top of the bottle, indicating that the sima is ready to drink. In warm weather this may take only about 8 hours. *Serve chilled.*

Makes 8 pints or 4 quarts of beverage

Sunset Magazine

In the fall of 1961, immediately after returning from our year in Finland, Dick accepted an assistantship at Stanford to work on his PhD in geology. As we drove into Palo Alto, through Menlo Park, my heart leapt into my throat as we turned the corner toward Stanford Village, which was to be our home for the next three years. On that corner was a low-slung, lovely building surrounded by beautifully landscaped trees, shrubs, and flowers with the *Sunset* logo on the front. It was the most exotic setting I had ever seen!

The building in which *Sunset* magazine was housed was designed by Cliff May, a California architect best known for developing the postwar "dream home"—a ranch-style house with an indoor–outdoor feel, embracing the environment where the sun shines three hundred-plus days a year. The *Sunset* offices had a comfortable atmosphere, and even though each department was housed in a different "corner" of the open space, there remained a lot of privacy in the open office, and sounds didn't carry from one desk to another.

I had been introduced to *Sunset* during the summer I worked as the cook at the elegant Sunshine Lake estate north of Duluth that belonged to Mrs. Whitney. *Sunset* at that time was available only for the western market, and it was an upscale publication with excellent, innovative food stories with recipes that were very well written and triple tested. I could never have imagined that I would have a chance at working for the magazine—my absolute dream job.

The assistantship Dick had been offered at Stanford covered only his expenses, so I knew I had to get a job. The next day I inquired about employment at *Sunset* and found that the food department needed a typist. I was so excited! I had the required degree in home economics, so I applied for and landed the job. It was like a dream come true.

I was given a desk and typewriter, plus an "in" and "out" basket into which the writers placed the rough copies of their stories and recipes. Within a month or two there was a vacancy within the department and I was promoted into the position of writer. I felt like the luckiest person in the world.

By typing the stories of the professionals in the department, I learned how to write recipes. It was wonderful on-the-job training. The pay—along with leftovers from the test kitchen—was enough to keep the family fed.

It was so exciting to be included in the planning meetings. I had ideas for zillions of stories, and soon I was given permission to write stories. What a thrill! In every planning session I threw out at least a half dozen ideas that were appropriate for the upcoming issue.

Even though there were demands not only from my student husband but also from our three- and five-year old children, I didn't mind it because I was living my dream at *Sunset*. It was the kind of job I had lusted for—the opportunity of a lifetime.

It was exciting to handle original typewritten copy by Helen Evans Brown, the revered culinary authority of the West Coast during the 1950s and 1960s. Her writing was always compelling and her ideas were fresh and new. Our policy was to test each recipe three times, and I felt honored to take hers into the *Sunset* test kitchens.

We had just returned from a year in Helsinki and I was pumped. Dick was spending long hours in the geology department at Stanford and the kids were pooped after spending their days tearing around University Village under the watchful eye of a neighbor who, of course, I paid by the hour. They were in bed early, so I usually had the evening to myself.

At the same time, I had my boxful of notes and recipes from Finland to work on in the evenings and on weekends. Going through what I had gathered in Finland was fun. From that work, I presented the idea for my first book, *The Finnish Cookbook*, to Proctor Melquist, the editor in chief of *Sunset*. But it wasn't the type of book the magazine's parent company, Lane Publishing, would publish. However, Proc had connections in New York. We presented the idea and eventually Herbert Michelman at Crown Publishers was enthusiastic and wanted to add my book to Crown's international cook-book series. It was first published in 1964 and is still in print these many years later.

A Marriage Encounter with Moussaka

My new husband was a very picky eater. Pasta was out. So was rice. He was a meat-and-potatoes guy. In fact, I was told that the hot lunch cooks at Warba would save food for Dick if they knew the menu the next day would include something he didn't like—like Spanish rice or spaghetti.

Moussaka

This is an adaptation of the recipe we used at *Sunset*. I make this today with the ground lamb from our son Greg's farm in Missouri.

2 tablespoons butter
2 tablespoons olive oil
2 large eggplants (2½ to 3 pounds total) cut into ½-inch thick slices
2 pounds lean ground lamb
2 large onions, chopped
2 cloves garlic, minced
2 tablespoons flour
1 teaspoon each ground cinnamon, oregano, and salt
½ teaspoon each nutmeg and pepper
½ cup each tomato catsup and water
¾ cup dry red wine
1 can (about 15 ounces) Italian-style tomatoes, drained (save liquid)
    and chopped
½ cup minced parsley

Custard Topping

½ cup (1 stick) butter
½ cup all-purpose flour
4 cups milk
6 eggs
¼ teaspoon each ground nutmeg and white pepper
2½ cups grated Parmesan or hard Greek cheese

Still, little by little, he became more adventurous. While traveling in Italy, we stopped in Rome, hoping to tour the catacombs, the underground tunnels that were used to bury bodies along the Old Appian Way. I think we were attracted to the area because we knew of pizza mixes that were titled "Appian Way." We had to wait an hour or so for the attraction to open, so we found an outdoor café in the meantime. We were served the most delicious veal-stuffed cannelloni with a creamy Parmesan sauce that completely changed Dick's mind about pasta. At another meal in Rome, a deep plate of lemon risotto changed his long-standing opinion about rice. But the last thing to go was his total disdain for lamb.

When I was on the staff at *Sunset*, we were doing a feature story on lamb and I brought food home from the test kitchen for dinner every night for a

Preheat the oven to 400°F. Divide the butter and oil evenly between 2 large rimmed baking pans. Place the pans in the oven as it is preheating and tilt the pans to distribute the mixture evenly. Arrange the eggplant slices in a single layer in the pans and turn to coat with the butter-and-oil mixture. Bake, uncovered, for 15 minutes, turning the eggplant slices once. Continue baking for 15 minutes more until the eggplant is soft. Drain the eggplant slices on paper towels.

Crumble the lamb into a wide frying pan over medium-high heat. Add onions and garlic and cook, stirring often, until onions are soft. Spoon off and discard the excess fat.

Stir in the flour, cinnamon, oregano, salt, nutmeg, and pepper. Slowly stir in the catsup, water, wine, tomatoes with the liquid, and parsley. Cook, stirring, until thick, about 15 minutes; set aside.

For the custard topping, melt the butter and stir in the flour; cook, stirring, until bubbly. Gradually stir in the milk and cook, stirring, until bubbly and thickened. Beat the eggs with the nutmeg and pepper. Gradually stir in 1 cup of the hot white sauce; then pour the egg mixture into the remaining white sauce. Cook, stirring constantly, for 1 minute. Remove from the heat and stir in the cheese.

Arrange half the cooked eggplant in a greased 9- by 13-inch baking dish; evenly spread with the meat sauce and top with the remaining eggplant. Spread the custard topping evenly over all. (At this point you may let cool, then cover and refrigerate the dish until the next day.)

Bake in the 350°F oven, uncovered, for 50 minutes or 1 hour if refrigerated, or until the custard is bubbly at the edges and center feel firm. Cut into squares to serve.

Makes 8 to 10 servings

week. I told him it was veal, and he devoured it. The following weekend, we were invited to a friend's home for dinner. She had prepared moussaka. My husband, of course, asked what was in it.

When he was told the ingredients, he responded that he didn't eat lamb. That's when I let him in on my secret; he'd been eating lamb all week. The moussaka was delicious, and better than that, it was the last breakthrough into a whole world of food acceptance. Today, Dick will try anything—even a diet of breakfasts with no toast!

A Food Writer and a Mom

"Pull up my pants, wipe my nose, and make cookies!" That was what my three-year-old son, Greg, said pretty much every day when I stepped into our apartment at Stanford Village after spending the day working at *Sunset*. I really wanted to be a good mom, so I made cookies.

Cathy, who was five when we moved to California, entered kindergarten at the Laurel School, a public school in the Atherton School District, smack in the middle of a wealthy and prestigious community. Shirley Temple Black and her family resided there.

Cathy always was very self-confident and shrugged off comments made by other kids about her lack of "designer" tennis shoes and dresses. One weekend she was invited to the birthday party of one of her wealthy friends. The mother phoned me and said that they really wanted Cathy to attend the party but she didn't have to bring a gift.

Greg (age three) and Cathy (age five) outside our home in Stanford Village.

When I dropped her off at the home of her friend, her friend ran out to meet her and asked her where her gift was. Cathy just replied, "I didn't bring one," and confidently entered the scene of the party. It was a catered affair, with cloth-covered tables, multicolored umbrellas, and pretty lights strung over the backyard. The pile of gifts was at least six feet deep. Later, when Cathy returned home, she described all the gifts—it sounded like her friend received one of every item in the toy department!

Jumbo Sugar Jumbles

This is a simple drop sugar cookie that dates back to the 1800s and is the kind of simple cookie I would often make for the family. I included this recipe in my *Great Holiday Baking Book*, originally published by Clarkson Potter in 1994 and republished by the University of Minnesota Press in 2001.

½ cup (1 stick) butter, at room temperature
½ cup sugar
1 large egg
1½ cups all-purpose flour
¼ teaspoon baking soda
¼ teaspoon salt
Water and sugar, for dipping

Preheat the oven to 375°F. Lightly grease a cookie sheet, or cover with parchment paper.

In a large bowl with an electric mixer, cream the butter and sugar together well. Add the egg and beat until light.

Stir the flour, baking soda, and salt together and then add it to the creamed mixture; mix until the dough is stiff.

Using a large ice-cream scoop, divide the dough into equal-sized mounds, placing them 3 inches apart on the prepared pan. For normal-sized cookies, cut the big mounds in half. Flatten with a fork dipped in water and then in sugar.

Bake for 12 to 15 minutes until light golden brown. Remove from the oven and cool on a wire rack.

Makes 6 jumbo cookies or 12 normal-sized cookies

Welcome Back to Duluth

"You're such a hot-shot home economist, tell me what makes good food." Red faced, my new boss pointed at me, practically spitting the words.

As they say about death, my life flashed before me. That summer we had relocated back to Duluth, where Dick, with his newly acquired PhD from Stanford, had accepted a position at the University of Minnesota Duluth in the geology department. I had tearfully left the job of my dreams in California as a food writer for *Sunset* magazine, the journal of western living. I had started as a typist three years earlier and quickly climbed to the position of full-time staff writer. It was the job I had always wanted, and just as my pay was about to climb to the next level, we had to leave. It was 1964 and I hadn't even considered the option of divorce.

Dick and I had packed our worldly belongings into the back of our tan 1956 VW Beetle, leaving just enough room for our two kids, six-year-old Cathy and four-year-old Greg, to lie flat on their stomachs on top of the pile as we drove and camped our way from California to Minnesota. Today, of course, such travel with kids would be illegal. We had shipped our books by mail, and we also had an ailing Ford Anglia, the British version of a small Ford car, that barely made it up the mountains. It was packed with our tent, sleeping bags, and food. We each drove one of our cars. I was thirty years old.

Before I left, a kindly editor at *Sunset* had suggested that in Duluth there was a company called Chun King that was owned by a man named Jeno Paulucci. I wrote the name into my date book and checked into Chun King, a very successful line of canned Chinese-like food products (chow mein and chop suey), as soon as we were settled in our new home. Not only did we need the money, but I also needed to fulfill my dreams. Thus began my search for something that was as fun as working for the magazine of western living.

I applied for a job at Chun King and was hired on the spot as a product developer in the research and development department. In the first hour of my job, I saw Jeno Paulucci himself, the president and owner of Chun King, subject a group of employees to an uncontrolled outburst. Shouting profanities, the red-faced big boss began throwing deep-fried chicken legs at the wall of the test kitchen while stunned food techs looked on.

When he spat his anger toward me, my inner calm took over even though

I was surprised by the unexpected explosiveness of his demand that I tell him what made good food. I remember thinking that the answer was simple and I replied, "Well, first you have to start with good ingredients and a good idea, and then, not wreck the food with bad preparation techniques." He had no answer to that.

The two dozen foil containers of reheated "Chinese" food that were laid out on the counter were entirely unknown to me, a brand-new employee. I was the only woman in the room and felt embarrassed for everyone who witnessed this tirade, and I thought that for sure Hot Head would regret his behavior once he settled down. I started to slip out of the kitchen as the vulgarities continued.

He noticed me leaving. I felt a hand grip my arm. "You're going to get a bath in this along with everybody else!" he said, as he pulled me back into the room. I stood there, silent and a bit puzzled, as the attack went on.

The bizarre event I was seeing was called a "cutting"—a new term to me. It referred to the process of tasting and evaluating new product ideas. Jeno always had another entrepreneurial idea in mind. This time it was for a new chain of fast-food restaurants that was to be called the Chop Chop House. The plan was to serve Asian-style food quickly (*Chop chop!*) to the public. The customer would place an order, and the food would be delivered in minutes, hot and ready for takeout. The techs in the kitchen had gone to work creating frozen foods that they thought would fit the theme.

So the foods on display that day had all been prepared, packaged, frozen, and reheated for evaluation—just as they would be before being served at one of the future restaurants. The selections included Middle America's versions of sweet and sour pork and chicken, fried chicken legs, teriyaki beef, Chinese shrimp, stir-fried vegetables, fried rice, chop suey, and chow mein, among other unremarkable choices. The list read like the canned foods section in a supermarket at the time. I knew nothing about the idea until I was ordered into the cutting. Chop Chop House never made it from the concept stage to reality.

The "research lab" at Chun King was in reality nothing more than a huge, square kitchen with laminate countertops set along the walls and down the center of a rather dull and lifeless flat-white space illuminated by fluorescent lighting. There were occasional sinks and home-style, outdated kitchen ranges and a series of plug-ins on the walls. If everybody plugged a fry pan or deep fryer into the 110-volt outlets at the same time, the circuits blew. I felt out of place with the all-male staff in this ill-planned company kitchen.

The crew was friendly enough, but at coffee break, everybody—including women—lit up cigarettes and I could hardly breathe. I watched a sweet young secretary go from borrowing a puff from a friend's Pall Mall to bumming cigarettes to smoking from her own pack.

After six months in the Chun King plant in the west end of Duluth, I proposed that I switch to a per project, hourly basis and instead work out of my home kitchen. They liked my idea and I transferred my product development duties to my own kitchen. It was such a relief.

Months later, when Jeno was making plans to sell his Chun King company to R. J. Reynolds, he knew he wanted to retain the rights to the highly successful egg roll technology that he had had developed. In fact, it was actually my own kid brother Eugene who had been hired as an engineer to develop the machine that would automatically extrude fillings onto a continuous sheet of egg roll skin, then fold, seal, and cut the product into little pillows. The idea was to develop a line of snack food products for a new company once Chun King had been sold.

While I was working in my own kitchen, I got a call from the vice president in charge of new product development. He asked me to come up with as many new fillings for the egg roll as I could, and he indicated that they did not have to be Asian or "Chinese."

Fun project. I purchased four-inch square wonton skins for the project and, brainstorming by myself, came up with fifty-five different ideas for fillings that I thought would appeal to the general public. I started out with popular sandwich fillings like cheeseburger, California burger, Reuben sandwich fillings, even peanut butter and jelly—because I was told that the boss really liked his PB & J sandwiches. Five or six of the fillings were "pizza" flavored, made with Italian sausage, pepperoni, or shrimp, while some of the others included Asian-style ingredients. I made the fillings, noted and recorded their ingredients carefully, sealed them all in egg roll skins, and froze them. To serve, they would simply be reheated in the oven or deep fryer.

The cutting for the egg rolls was to be held later that summer on the grand personal estate belonging to Paulucci, situated on Lake Kabetogama—one of the most beautiful lakes in northern Minnesota. I had two weeks to come up with ideas and product samples. With my prototypes all sealed, packaged, and labeled in the freezer—two dozen of each of the fifty-five flavors—I made the deadline.

On a sunny July morning I was picked up in Duluth by the company plane. We flew north for about forty-five minutes and landed on the still, clear blue waters of one of the grandest lakes in our North Country, in front of the sprawling estate that looked more like a resort than a private home. We unloaded the cooler of frozen egg roll prototypes and toted them into the industrial-sized kitchen of the mansion.

I donned my whites and heated up the commercial-sized deep fryer in the modern, all-stainless kitchen. There were two assistants clothed in white jackets to help me. We didn't talk much as I wrote out little signs noting the fillings and began cooking the prototype egg rolls.

Around the massive, polished mahogany conference table sat a dozen serious-faced executives in their dark suits, white shirts, and ties. They tasted and evaluated round after round of egg rolls with new fillings. The tastings were headed up by Jeno himself. When the "pizza"-filled egg rolls appeared, the conversation stopped. The other fillings were irrelevant. "That's it!" he shouted. "Jeno's Pizza Rolls" were born. The excitement was palpable.

The following week I asked for a twenty-five-cent raise, from $3.50 to $3.75 per hour. The response? "Please don't ask for that! We can't afford it."

Some years later, Paulucci (the hot head) sold his Jeno's Pizza Rolls brand to the Pillsbury Corporation for $135 million. He died in 2011 at the age of ninety-three. The last time I checked, his $100 million estate was still in litigation. Jeno's Pizza Rolls are now sold under the brand name of Totino's.

The moral of this story? "We come into this world with nothing. We leave with nothing."

When people tell me I should have protested and insisted on more money, all I can do is refer to the biblical story of the workers in the vineyard. I agreed to work for a certain amount, and that is what I received. No more, no less.

Somebody's House

In California restaurants abounded, and my job as a food editor at *Sunset* had planted seeds of optimism and curiosity about starting a restaurant of my own. I was excited at the idea of opening a Scandinavian restaurant in Duluth, especially after we had some lively discussions with a group of friends. (Duluth could still use a Scandinavian restaurant!)

One of our group immediately got busy looking for a building or site for our restaurant, which at the time was still nameless. All fired up, he found a building one day at the Mount Royal shopping center that was up for rent. It had been a restaurant called the Royal Inn and wasn't far from the University of Minnesota Duluth campus.

When I inspected the facility, I found that the kitchen consisted of an open-topped gas-fired broiler and a refrigerator. Nothing else. It was obviously not a candidate for a Scandinavian restaurant, which would have required more space in the kitchen, more cooking stations, and better storage. It wasn't a good deal, but we signed anyway.

Once the deal was made, I wrote the menu almost overnight. The basic idea was a variety of different burgers served open-faced on slices of home-made bread.

We met one evening shortly afterward at our house. The party consisted of two lawyers and their wives, our partner and his wife, Dick and myself. I had made sourdough bread, shaped one-third-pound hamburgers ready for grilling, and prepared a variety of sauces and toppings for the burgers. We called them "dinnerburgers."

We started that night with the simple "Cannibalburger"—a smallish patty of raw lean meat, uncooked, with capers, parsley, anchovy strips, topped with a raw egg yolk, a version of the classic French steak tartare. There was the "Saunaburger": served nude, with nothing on the patty resting on a toasted bun, with a "switch" of parsley, salad, and garnish in just the appropriate places. The "Duluth Blizzardburger" had a "drift" of sour cream on top. I had dubbed a cheese-topped variety the "Berwegerburger"—and later had to ask the cheesemakers, the Berwegers in the nearby village of Meadowlands, for permission to use the name. They declined, saying, "Why don't you think of your own original name?" That one became the "Cheddarburger." After that I got creative. We had the "Tyroleanburger," topped with a sauce flavored with sap sago cheese, which sent the local food vendor we were using scrambling for a source. We later had to scratch that idea because the USDA had condemned sap sago due to the fact it was imported and had unprocessed herbs as its flavoring.

In the discussion that followed as we grilled and tasted our burgers, it emerged that we did not yet have a name for the restaurant. That was a problem. The brick-walled building sat on a hill at one end of a small shopping area and had a low-slung roof, no basement, and lots of big picture windows. One of us remarked that the building looked like somebody's house.

"That's it!" was the response. "We'll call it 'Somebody's House'!" At that time, Duluth had the Hilltop House, the Sweden House, and a number of other "houses."

We had no budget for advertising, yet Somebody's House quickly became the talk of the town.

People would say, "Let's go to Somebody's House for dinner." The inevitable response would be: "Whose house?"

We hired college students to do the cooking, serving, cleaning, and hosting for our guests. We hired my brother-in-law, Jack LaVoy, to be the manager. Things went along swimmingly. I handled ordering the food; Dick took care of the payroll—a complicated job with some forty-plus people on the payroll. One significant hire that we made was a UMD football star named Gary Doty, who later became the mayor of Duluth.

At the beginning of each school year, we'd notice that the supply of dishes and silverware had diminished. Apparently, we were furnishing dorm rooms

Our restaurant, Somebody's House, in Duluth.

Cathy, age thirteen, in her confirmation robe. Greg, eleven, is dressed for the occasion; Susanna is two. Autumn 1971.

with necessities that were "lifted" a piece at a time by some of the employees and guests. There was also the typical pilfering of food items, none of it done maliciously, but with the innocent thought that "just one doesn't make a difference."

To standardize the menu items, I wrote out recipes for each of the sauces that were to top the various burgers. One of our "chefs," Don, loved to put his own personal touch on things—so he began tasting the sauces. That was okay, except for the "Fireburger." This burger sauce was spiced with Tabasco, and each day, Don added a little more of the hot sauce until customers began complaining about the fire in the fireburger. We were ordering Tabasco sauce by the case every week!

Analyzing the situation, I came to realize that the human taster gets accustomed to the heat of peppers. Eventually Don's additions to the sauce made it so hot it nearly "blew the tops" off several customers' heads. To correct the situation, the chefs were ordered to follow the recipes, *not* their tongues!

Many of our burgers became customer favorites: the "Norskburger" was topped with a sauce made with gjetost cheese; the "Beatleburger" was topped with a "wig" of coleslaw; the "Mushroom Burger" was topped with a mushroom sauce; the "Great Dane" was topped with a fried egg, tomatoes, and cucumbers—and so the menu read, with two and a half dozen more "creative" burgers. The prices seem amazing to me today—they ranged from 85 cents to $1.50.

One that intrigued most everyone was the "Dareburger"—and I thought nobody would order it, but only talk about it. The description read: "The hamburger topped with vanilla ice cream, hot chocolate sauce, nuts, and a cherry." The first to order this weird combo was an elderly banker, a gentleman who later became a regular customer. He asked for more chocolate sauce!

Eventually we decided that it was too much to handle. Our third child, Susanna, was a newborn and our two older children were in junior high. I found it difficult to concentrate on much more than just taking care of family affairs. Dick was teaching full-time at the University of Minnesota Duluth. Our payroll costs were high, so our profit-and-loss statement did not look good. We ended up selling the restaurant to two families for basically what we had put into the operation. They continued to run Somebody's House for several years and were comfortably happy with their lives.

What follows are recipes for a few of the most popular items on the Somebody's House menu.

Rabbitburger

This was a standby on the old Somebody's House menu. The sauce is made with a richly flavored sharp cheddar cheese and beer; known as Welsh rarebit, the sauce also is delicious served over toast.

2 cups (8 ounces) shredded sharp cheddar cheese
2 teaspoons cornstarch
½ teaspoon dry mustard
½ cup flat beer
1 teaspoon Worcestershire sauce
Freshly ground black pepper
Grilled 1-inch-thick Italian or French bread or a large hamburger bun
Grilled meat patties, beef, turkey, or vegetable, done to your liking
Sliced fresh tomatoes
Garnish of a sprig of fresh rosemary, thyme, or parsley

In a bowl, toss the cheese with the cornstarch and mustard.

Combine the beer and Worcestershire sauce in a saucepan and heat until simmering. Stir in the cheese mixture until cheese is melted. Add the pepper.

Top the bread with a grilled burger and a slice of fresh tomato. Spoon the sauce over.

Garnish with a sprig of herb.

Makes about 2½ cups sauce, enough for about 8 burgers

Stroganoff Burger

A creamy mushroom sauce is delicious on a char-grilled burger. You also can place the burger on top of cooked egg noodles and then spoon the sauce over the whole works.

2 tablespoons butter or canola oil
8 ounces sliced fresh mushrooms
1 medium-sized sweet onion, finely chopped
1 can (10.5-ounce) undiluted beef broth
1 cup dairy sour cream
1 can (8-ounce) tomato sauce
1 tablespoon Worcestershire sauce
Grilled 1-inch-thick Italian or French bread or a large hamburger bun
Grilled meat patties, beef, turkey, or vegetable, done to your liking
Sliced pickled beets for garnish
Sprigs of dill for garnish

Heat the butter or oil in a skillet and add the mushrooms and onion. Cook over medium heat until just softened, about 2 minutes, stirring often. Add the broth, sour cream, tomato sauce, and Worcestershire sauce. Cook over high heat until slightly thickened, about 2 to 3 minutes. Top the bread with a grilled burger and spoon the sauce over. Garnish with sliced pickled beets and a sprig of fresh dill.

Makes 6 servings

Swiss Fondue

Imported Swiss Gruyère melts into a pale, smooth, creamy sauce. For the cheese to melt well, it must be aged or the sauce will be grainy and not homogeneous.

4 tablespoons butter
3 tablespoons all-purpose flour
1½ cups milk
½ cup shredded Gruyère, aged Swiss, or Asiago cheese
Pinch cayenne pepper
Pinch nutmeg
Salt and pepper to taste

Melt the butter in a heavy saucepan and add the flour. Slowly stir in the milk and whisk until thickened. Stir in the cheese until melted. Season with cayenne pepper, nutmeg, salt, and pepper. Serve with bread cubes to dip into the sauce.

Makes about 2 cups sauce, enough for two generous servings

Jeno and the Big Idea

About 4:00 A.M. one day in late 1969 we got a phone call from Jeno Paulucci. He had the idea of making a franchise out of the Somebody's House restaurant concept. Of course, he didn't want to buy the local store, as we had yet to turn a profit. We explained that that was because neither Dick nor I could spend much time at the restaurant.

Our involvement with Somebody's House for the most part was limited to checking the place first thing on Sunday morning before going to church and refilling supplies that were needed. Saturday nights were always busy, and we often ran out of basics like ground meat, French fries, and lettuce.

The restaurant did not have adequate refrigeration to stock up in preparation for busy weekends, so we were on a first-name basis with the local restaurant supply house and our favorite butcher. Somebody's House opened at 10:00 A.M. and ran until midnight. We made our own bread that we called "penny loaves"; they were sliced thick to form the base for the burgers and to accompany other items on the menu.

Jeno's check to us for one dollar to franchise Somebody's House, with his note "Only Seed I Hope!"

Jeno, of course, couldn't factor tasks like these into his idea of running a restaurant, but he did want to buy the name and basic idea from us. We haggled back and forth for a few weeks, each of us saying that the other cut a hard deal. In the end, we agreed to 222,222 shares in the new company. To seal the deal, Jeno gave us a check for one dollar and a crisp one-dollar bill. I framed them both.

The check and a buck were to sell him the name and the idea. I was to be a vice president in charge of menu development. But I didn't hear anything from Jeno and his company after that. A local restaurateur was hired to do what I thought I'd be doing. The prototype restaurant that they built in south Minneapolis failed miserably. They had not followed any of our recommendations, plus the guys Jeno hired bought used equipment at the same price as new, which cost the company dearly. They were $100,000 in debt after the first year. What a flop.

We were paid a penny a share for our stock, which amounted to a check for $2,222.22. So much for that!

I was never much of a businessperson. Nor was Dick, even though he almost graduated with a business degree from UMD before switching his major to geology.

One year, I asked him about his marketing classes—what did he remember from them?

His answer was two words: Adam's Hats.

Two Years at Vocational School

In 1971 I was approached by the Duluth School Board to take a position teaching post–high school students quantity cooking at the Duluth Area Vocational Technical Institute (it is now Lake Superior College and is part of the Minnesota State Colleges and Universities system).

I accepted the position, but while negotiating my salary I was told that I didn't need as much money because I was a woman with a husband working full-time at the university and that I was not eligible for the benefits package. I would have to start at a minimal salary. Never mind that I had to drive to the school, sometimes work late into the evening because I was in charge of special events, and that I had babysitting expenses.

Nonetheless, I was excited to put some of my teaching skills to work. My goal was to raise the quality of restaurant foods in Duluth.

I shared my work space with the bakery classes that were taught by Dexter Larson, an experienced and affable commercial baker. We taught our classes in one large room full of commercial-sized mixers, sheeters, worktables, and large walk-in coolers. Dexter had been teaching for two years and had worked up a very respectable reputation for his Danish pastry, breads of all kinds, cookies, cakes, and doughnuts.

My job, it turned out, was to provide food for the school cafeteria—it was somebody's idea of the "perfect" application of the principles of quantity cookery. I was to plan the menus, order the ingredients, and have my students prepare the food for sale. We could not lose money, I was told, so what we took in during the lunch hour had to balance what I spent on ingredients.

The curriculum was to include menu planning, determining food costs, sanitation, meat cutting, and the major techniques of preparation, such as baking, roasting, braising, and broiling. The challenge each day was to provide food that would be sold in the cafeteria at noon to the student body. Needless to say, students did not necessarily have sophisticated tastes.

Besides quantity food preparation and baking, the institute taught various technical courses such as auto mechanics, electrics, architecture, secretarial, and nursing—and I was told "if they can't handle any of that, they can always cook." So my class turned out to be an interesting group of characters. There were a couple of serious students and then there were those who showed up hungover in the morning. It was also the beginning of the "druggie" era in Duluth. A couple of students would arrive so high I was afraid they'd fly into an open oven door! More than one student required an excessive amount of individual attention. Because they varied so much in previous cooking and food experience, I tried to match their skills with their abilities and then determine when they were ready to individually take on more skilled jobs.

Sometimes they would try to get creative: "Teach!" one student questioned as he displayed his creation, "other than looks, taste, and texture, what do you think of it?"

Karjalan Paisti (Karelian Three-Meat Stew)

This has been a favorite "go-to" carnivorous main course for a big party. It is really a "recipeless" recipe for a delicious long-roasted stew. I often simply calculate the amount of meat we need based on the number of people we need to serve, figuring on 3 to 4 servings per pound. Then, I figure on about ½ teaspoon salt per pound and an equal weight of sliced onions. As I put it together, I strew in whole allspice and/or whole peppercorns, about a tablespoonful of one or the other (sometimes both). I like to serve this over cooked wild rice, but Dick prefers mashed potatoes. So I offer both. The great thing about this stew is that I can get it ready a day in advance and shove it into a slow oven to roast to juicy succulence in 6 to 8 hours. In my mind, the longer, the better. Oh, and it needs to be cooked in a heavy cast-iron or enameled cast-iron pot to retain the juices.

> 1½ pounds beef stew meat, cut into 1-inch cubes
> 1½ pounds boneless pork, cut into 1-inch cubes
> 1½ pounds boneless lamb, cut into 1-inch cubes
> 4½ to 5 pounds onions, quartered and sliced ¼ inch thick
> About 4 teaspoons salt
> About 1 tablespoon whole allspice or black peppercorns

Layer the meats with the onions in a heavy 3- to 5-quart casserole or Dutch oven with a tight-fitting lid. Sprinkle the meat with the salt and allspice as you go. Cut a piece of parchment paper large enough to cover the entire mixture in the pot, pressing the meats down firmly and tucking the paper down around the edges tightly. Cover with the lid and place in a slow oven, 275°F for 6 to 8 hours or until the meat is very tender. To serve, spoon over mashed potatoes or wild rice.

Makes about 12 servings

I learned to love them all, even though it was a challenge to accomplish the production every day. Planning quantity menus, ordering the ingredients, and handling the cost of the food served kept me busy daily in the hours after school let out at 4:30. On top of it all, we were expected to plan a couple of major event dinners that were open to the public. This provided me an opportunity to teach such things as ice sculpture, buffet presentation, and the plating of food. That we invited the public to our events added a few more tasks for my students (and me)—mainly advertising, designing dinner tickets, and then selling them. The sale of tickets helped our bottom line, and the students enjoyed these opportunities to "show off" their accomplishments.

After two school years, I was totally exhausted and quit my job. The school board hired two men in my place. I bet they each got twice my salary!

Cooking School in the South of France with Simca

When I found I could enroll in a week of classes with Simone Beck, the renowned French chef and cookbook author also known as Simca, I was truly excited. I had gathered enough frequent flyer miles and saved enough money to apply for admission and cover my airfare to and from France.

After writing to Simca and confirming dates, I committed to a week in her kitchen. I was so thrilled, and anticipation covered the days and weeks before I left. When the day to leave finally arrived, it felt unreal. I had so many mixed emotions. I felt like I was deserting those who needed me at home. I felt a little selfish for taking the time and the money for this trip. Yet I felt privileged that I could go, in spite of the fact that I had to rely on credit cards for incidental expenses. I prayed for lots of inspiration to come to me because of the trip.

Simca and her husband, Jean Fischbacher, met me and another cooking student named Geraldine at Charles de Gaulle Airport. Bags safely in the trunk of their car, we had a hair-raising ride through the winding roads and villages to Bramafan in Provence, where La Pitchoune (the "little one") sat with its red tile roof and white stucco exterior. This was to be our home for the next few days. Our quarters and the instruction kitchen were in "La Campanette," a nearby five-year-old building made to house cooking school students such as us.

We were greeted with a tray of snack bits, little radishes, and one-inch squares of duck pâté. This was going to be a week of fabulous eating. After the snack, we were given a lunch of a gratin of celeriac and potatoes, French bread with sweet butter and home-cured olives, terrine of pork, and a green salad. Dead tired from the overnight flight and feeling like a zombie, after we ate I plopped onto the bed in the room assigned to me. Even though I hated to miss a beautiful afternoon, I slept for almost three hours. When I awoke, we were invited to the château for a raspberry aperitif and sandwiches of prosciutto on large croutons spread with mustard.

What followed was a planning session for the week ahead. On Monday we boned chicken, stuffed and rolled it, and made pastries (pâté brisée) for quiches and tarts. And that was just Monday. All the steps were worked out in great detail. Because I didn't speak French, Geraldine, who could, captured Simca's attention. That was fine with me, as I had time to observe and realize that there was nothing really new to me in any of the lessons.

The kitchen assistant, Jeanette, was a funny, fat, squat little lady who wore tennis shoes and chewed on a violet stem all the time, the blossom end drooping from her mouth. I was totally entertained as I observed the dynamics of the characters in the kitchen. When I'd ask a question, Simca faced Geraldine to give the answer. Jeanette, who spoke no English, was kind and never wrong about anything. Geraldine kowtowed to Simca, and I was like a fence post in the corner, soaking it all in.

Tarte de Nancy

This special almond dessert tart was a specialty of Simone Beck's. It is kind of sweet and rich, so I like to serve it in very small pieces. The white wine gives a nice, flaky texture to the pastry. If you prefer, you can substitute fresh lemon juice.

1 recipe pâté sucrée (recipe follows)
5 heaping tablespoons apricot jam
2 eggs, separated
1 cup sugar
¾ cup pulverized toasted almonds
½ teaspoon vanilla
3 tablespoons milk
Pinch of salt
Powdered sugar

Make the pastry and line an 8- or 9-inch tart pan (preferably with removable bottom) with the pastry. Chill about 30 minutes.

Preheat the oven to 375°F. Spread the pastry with the jam and bake for 10 minutes. Put the egg whites into a separate bowl and the yolks into a saucepan (not aluminum). Gradually beat the sugar into the yolks, waiting after each addition until the mixture is runny before adding more sugar. Beat in the pulverized almonds, vanilla, and milk. Mixture will be very thick. Set over low heat, stirring, until sugar has melted. Beat the egg whites with a pinch of salt until stiff but not dry. Stir a bit of the whites into the yolk mixture; then fold all back into the whites. Fill the tart shell with this almond cream. Bake for 18 minutes until top is puffed and browned. Remove from the oven and sprinkle with powdered sugar. Increase oven heat to 450°F and bake until the sugar is lightly caramelized.

Makes about 8 servings

Pâté Sucrée

This is a very slightly sweetened butter pastry that is ideal for a dessert tart, as it isn't really sweet but makes the flavors blend well.

½ cup (1 stick) chilled butter, preferably unsalted, plus 1 tablespoon more
1½ cups all-purpose flour
¼ teaspoon salt
2 tablespoons sugar
1 egg, slightly beaten
1 tablespoon white wine or lemon juice
3 to 5 tablespoons ice water

Cut the butter into tiny bits and drop into bowl containing the flour, salt, and sugar. Using a pastry blender, two knives, or a pastry fork, cut in butter until the mixture resembles dry oatmeal. Be careful not to overblend. Beat the egg, white wine or lemon juice, and 3 tablespoons of the ice water together using a fork. Make a well in the flour mixture and stir in the egg mixture. Stir with a fork until flour is moistened and add a tablespoon or so more water if necessary. Press mixture into a ball. Flour the heel of your hand and knead lightly just a few times. Wrap the pastry in foil or plastic wrap and chill 20 minutes. To line a tart shell, roll the pastry to about 1/8 inch thick, fit it into the pan, and trim to the edge of the pan.

We also traveled. We were taken shopping in nearby Cannes, and to St. Paul de Vence and Tourrettes-sur-Loup to visit two old medieval cities and to a little charcuterie in Plascassier to learn how to make chicken ballotine.

We made terrines, brioche with a pâte in the center, apple tart, tart de Nancy, and many other wonderful dishes based on pastry. We also prepared poached foie gras, quenelles, mousseline of fish, a terrine with macaroni and sorrel sauce, crème caramel, chocolate soufflé, stuffed sole paupiettes, among many other things.

The highlight of the week was a five-course dinner at Le Moulin de Mougins arranged for us by Simca and prepared by the world-famous chef Roger Vergé himself. He greeted us with a basket of truffles with an aroma so intoxicating, it is still implanted in my psyche. I slept that night with my hand perfumed by one of the prized truffles, a "food of the kings" that the chef had allowed me to hold. I didn't wash that hand until the next day. And the dinner was a bargain at 511 francs for the two of us.

Nice Is Nice

After spending the week cooking with Simone Beck in Bramafan, my plan was to then spend five days exploring the city of Nice, thirty kilometers to the south, and stay at a pension. The book *Europe on 5 Dollars a Day* had given high ratings to a pension near the center of the city. It was reasonable and convenient, so I reserved five days and paid about seventy-five dollars. The woman who ran the boardinghouse wanted money in hand before I could be admitted to the pension.

My overnight bag slung over my shoulder, map in hand, I carefully traced the route from the bus station. No problems so far. I arrived at the pension and, just as the book had said, it was smack in the center of the city. Overgrown shrubbery and an unmowed lawn surrounded the sprawling old white stucco house caged by a wooden picket fence.

A woman with sharp, beady eyes answered the doorbell and bid me come in. She introduced herself as Madame Michaud, collected my money, and handed me a big iron key with the instructions that I must absolutely turn that key in when I left, as it was the only one she had for the room. Fortunately, her English was quite fluent (perhaps from entertaining many American students), although she spoke with a heavy French accent.

She led me down a long, dark, musty corridor and opened the door to what was going to be my "home" for the next five days. A single lightbulb hung in the center of the ceiling in a room that had at least fourteen-foot-high walls. It was the only light in the room. The narrow bed was covered with a khaki wool blanket tucked in all around and sank in the center before I even sat on it. A big old armoire to the right and a chair were the extent of the furnishings. The bath was shared—actually, it was just a toilet and a sink.

Madame Michaud ordered me to put my pack into the armoire and follow her into the parlor for a cup of tea. "You must have tea at four every afternoon!" There was also breakfast starting at seven in the morning, and Madame would have been to the market well before that.

I wasn't much for tea, particularly when I saw the light film of grease floating on top of the liquid. The cup, too, felt greasy. I couldn't shake that image, especially since I had just had such a lovely time at the cooking school with Simca and the others.

"Oh," I exclaimed, "I write about food, and I will be eating even my breakfast at a café or bakery." She insisted that it would be far too expensive for me to do that and that I should do my cooking for lunch and dinner right there in her kitchen.

A glance at her kitchen convinced me otherwise. Greasy dishes, washed in cold water, drained in the rack on the sink. The more I saw, the more I knew it was not the place for me.

"Madame Michaud," I said politely, "I have changed my mind. I would like my money back. I don't think I can stay here."

"Oh, no!" she shouted angrily. "I cannot let you go! I cannot give your money back! After all, I could have rented the room many times, but I saved it for you. Besides, any place you could go is much too expensive!"

The next morning I left early and found a welcoming little café for coffee and croissants. Madame scolded me for being so wasteful when I could have had breakfast with her. I just shrugged and went out to explore the open market, the bakeries, the restaurants, and the food shops. I had a beautiful bowlful of bouillabaisse for dinner in an outdoor café and some fruity local wine.

When I arrived back at the pension at about 9:00 P.M., she was terribly upset. "Where have you been? I expected you for dinner!"

I didn't answer.

During that night I plotted my escape. I couldn't get my money back, and this old woman wasn't about to let me go kindly. Besides, I was beginning to itch from something that seemed to be crawling around in bed with me. The heck with the money.

I awoke early and watched for her to leave for the market. Then I made my escape. My bag packed, I ran around the corner from the house as fast as I could and headed for the Hotel Sofitel, which I had spotted the day before. I checked in at 8:00 A.M. and took a glorious, hot shower.

When dressing afterward, I felt something heavy in my pocket. It was the key to the room at Madame Michaud's!

What to do? I really didn't want to see her again. But I had promised to leave the key when I left, and I knew the only right thing to do was to return it. I just wanted to leave and never see the place again. But I gritted my teeth and made it back to the dumpy, old stucco house just in time to meet her on the front walk. I handed the key to her and without any explanation said I would not be returning. Without waiting for a reply, I turned on my heel and left.

Nice was actually quite nice after escaping from Madame Michaud. I was relieved and felt I could breathe freely once again, sitting in an outdoor café, watching bicycles whirling by, hearing the sound of drums and marching bands in the air. Nice was filled at that time with the celebration of the annual carnival—a season in France that has a long history with its oldest origins tied to ancient Rome. It was circus-like, filled with feasting, singing, and dancing, and similar to today's Mardi Gras celebrations in New Orleans. It is a time of revelry and abandonment prior to the forty days of Lent. There were people and dogs all around. People were eating socca (chickpea flour crepes) and drinking rosé wine from water glasses. I enjoyed a croque monsieur and lemon tea at 3:30 in the afternoon.

A Totally Untraditional Bouillabaisse

Sometimes I still dream about this aromatic fish and shellfish stew I enjoyed in an outdoor café in Nice. What makes a bouillabaisse in Provence different from other fish soups is the selection of herbs and spices in the broth; the bony local Mediterranean fish; the way the fish are added one at a time and brought to a boil; and the method of serving. The aromatic broth is served first in a soup plate with slices of bread and rouille; then the fish is served separately on a large platter or, more simply, the fish and broth are brought to the table separately and served together in large soup plates. A crispy French baguette and a chilled glass of white wine had saved the day for me. I've tried to reproduce it using local ingredients—and this is the best I can do!

Traditionally, a bowl of hot broth is served along with the cooked fish, which is placed, hot, on a platter. You spread a piece of toasted baguette with the rouille—which is a mayonnaise-like sauce, freshly made, flavored with saffron, garlic, and roasted red pepper. The baguette is then placed in the bottom of each individual soup bowl. Scoop the broth and fish pieces onto the baguette slice.

¼ cup olive oil
1 large sweet onion, thinly sliced
1 fennel or anise bulb, thinly sliced
4 shallots, thinly sliced
2 cloves garlic, minced
¼ cup Pernod
¼ cup dry white wine
2 Roma tomatoes, diced
1 bay leaf
1 pinch saffron
1 cup (8 ounces) clam juice
½ pound yellow potatoes, scrubbed and quartered
4 pounds boneless fish, including any combination of shrimp, salmon, tilapia, cod, mussels, and scallops

I didn't realize it, but the parade in Nice is one of the most elaborate parades anywhere and can last for two weeks or longer. There were musical and street performers along with dozens of floats decorated with giant papiermâché heads, each with the face of a different caricature. I stumbled on this celebration unknowingly, and darn it, my camera was broken. After miles of walking, I was exhausted and settled back in at the Sofitel, having realized that even though it was expensive, animal comforts help in a foreign land, especially when you're alone.

Rouille

1 pinch saffron
2 cloves garlic
1 roasted red pepper, seeded, cored, and quartered
1 slice white bread
1 egg yolk
1 teaspoon salt
½ cup olive oil
Toasted baguette slices

Heat the olive oil in a heavy-bottomed pot. Add the onion and the sliced fennel or anise root. Cook over medium heat, stirring, until translucent and tender. Add the shallots and garlic and cook until fragrant, about 2 to 3 minutes.

Add the Pernod and white wine. Bring to a simmer; add the tomatoes.

Add the bay leaf, saffron, clam juice, and potatoes. Simmer for 10 minutes.

Add the seafood and then water to cover. Bring to a boil and cook 5 to 10 minutes.

For the rouille, remove 2 tablespoons of the broth from the pot and add it to a blender. Add the saffron, garlic, and red pepper. Tear bread into the blender and pulse to combine. Drizzle in half of the olive oil, pulsing to blend. Add the egg yolk and drizzle in the remaining olive oil, pulsing all the while. Season to taste with salt.

Spread a toasted baguette slice with about 1 teaspoon of the rouille and place in the bottom of each soup bowl. Ladle the bouillabaisse over the top. Serve with the remaining rouille and additional toasted bread slices on the side.

The Seven-Course
Morel Festival Meal

We had heard about the special meals at a small restaurant in the town of Bayport, Minnesota, located east of the Twin Cities on the St. Croix River. So we made plans to attend the special Morel Festival Meal in Bayport.

The doors opened at 7:00 P.M. Our reservation was honored, and we selected a table in a quiet corner where we could see everything yet have privacy. Other guests silently selected their tables. Ice clinked in stemmed, sweaty glasses. The steam from the kitchen wafted over the dining room, emitting the wonderful woodsy aroma of morels that were to make their way into our every course.

Muffled conversations, candlelight. A quarter loaf of half-wheat bread came in a small basket that was broken and covered with a white napkin. A small crock with whipped butter flavored with morels appeared and was set beside the bread, the top scraped flat, perfectly even with the edges of the little pot. We spread the soft off-white, morel-flecked, whipped butter on torn chunks of the rustic bread.

Then the waiter appeared.

"Your wine selection?" He made the rounds asking the same question. The wines appeared on all the tables.

"The first course tonight," our waitperson declared, "will be an oriental morel salad made with shredded carrots, snow peas, sweet onion, shredded napa cabbage, with lettuce, rice noodles, soy sauce and sesame oil dressing, topped with deep-fried morels and chopped cashews." Arranged on a huge white plate, the salad itself was all of three inches in diameter. A thin strand of shredded napa cabbage dripped down my chin, and what the salad perhaps lacked in volume, it replaced with flavor.

A four-ounce cup of silky, creamy morel soup, its flavor exploding on my palate, left me wanting more. Our waiter whisked away the empty dishes.

An hour later, we'd finished the first course and the soup as well as the bread and the morel butter. Five puffs of potato gnocchi came next, arranged on a plate that had been first covered with a pureed sweet pea sauce and sprinkled with tiny bits of thin, salty Serrano ham, finely diced fried morels, and drizzled with earthy-scented truffle oil.

In another three-quarters of an hour a lovely plate, centered with about a quarter of a cup of Israeli couscous, which looked a little like dark whole tapioca, and mixed with sautéed sweetbreads and morels, was placed before our sleepy eyes. It was dramatically drizzled with a reduction of port wine and served alongside a tablespoonful of sautéed spinach.

After a few pours of wine, and two glasses of ice water, and another forty-five-minute gap between courses, we were served a thimbleful of mint sorbet as a palate cleanser.

Cream of Morel Soup

¾ pound fresh morels (more or less to taste and your hunting success)
½ of a large sweet onion
3 medium to small russet potatoes
2 cups water
2 tablespoons butter
Salt and pepper to taste
½ cup dry white wine
1 cup chicken stock
1 cup heavy cream

Clean and chop the morels. If they are buggy, place in a salt-and-water solution—2 tablespoons salt to 1 quart water—and refrigerate for an hour or two. Rinse, drain, and dry the morels. Chop the onion. Peel and halve potatoes. Add both to soup pot with the water. Boil moderately until tender, 20 to 30 minutes.

Place a 2- to 3-quart saucepan over a medium flame. Add morels and a few dashes of salt. Cook morels gently for about 15 minutes, making sure they do not dry out. Add a few dashes of wine at a time to keep moist. When nearly done, add additional dry white wine, turn up flame, and continue cooking until liquid is almost gone. Add chicken stock and stir until blended.

When potatoes and onions are tender, remove from heat and blend until smooth. Return to pot.

Add morel mix to potato/onion mixture and simmer very gently, stirring occasionally to avoid scorching. After about 5 to 10 minutes, add cream and salt and pepper to taste.

The evening wore on, and whispered voices became speaking voices, became loud voices as yet another bottle of wine was delivered to tables.

Another three-quarters of an hour passed before a medallion of pork tenderloin a full 2½ inches in diameter perched atop a spoonful of morel sauce and glazed with a raspberry coulis arrived. We polished that off in less than five minutes. By now the noise level in the restaurant was to the point where we had to shout across the table to hear each other.

Three spears of asparagus, arranged in a spoke pattern on a plate thinly glazed with a pureed morel sauce and garnished with a single cashew, arrived a half hour later. We asked for more bread.

A round table in the corner with three couples had already consumed four bottles of wine. We calculated the cost of their wine at about $450.

At last dessert came. Two ounces of morel and chocolate pots de crème in a dainty little ceramic cup on a huge white plate sprinkled with chopped mint and two raspberries artfully arranged. It was gone in three minutes.

A hundred and fifty dollars later we were finished. We unfolded our legs slowly, which seemed to be permanently bent after almost four hours of sitting. The whole company exited the restaurant at the same time. I heard somebody say, "Let's go to Burger King. I'm hungry!"

In the Kitchen with Julia Child

It was a quiet, ordinary early summer day in 1992 when the phone rang at our home in Duluth. I was out doing errands. My mother-in-law, who was visiting, picked up the phone and almost fainted when she heard the voice on the other end: "Hello, this is Julia Child. I'd like to speak with Beatrice."

When I stepped in the door about an hour later, a breathless mom-in-law practically screamed: "Julia Child called you and she sounded just like she does on TV!"

I dialed the number she had nervously scribbled down, and sure enough, it *was* Julia. She explained that she was working on a book with Dorie Greenspan called *Baking with Julia*, and she wanted to know if I would be interested in doing a half-hour television show with her. WOULD I?!? Do birds fly? Is the pope Catholic?

I still don't know exactly why I got to be so privileged, but what followed were intense discussions about the potential appearance on her show. What would I bake? How can I possibly show Julia Child something she didn't already know? Julia, with her matter-of-fact wisdom, assured me that nobody knows it all. There is always something new to be learned.

But me? "Yes, of course," she said. "I have your *Finnish Cookbook* and your *Scandinavian Baking Book* and have admired both of them very much." She went on to say that she has a special place in her heart for Norway, as she and her husband, Paul, had spent some years there.

After much discussion with the producers of the show, we finally settled on my version of a quick buttery Danish pastry and whole-grain Swedish hardtack. What followed were questions from me such as: "What should I wear? What do I need to bring with me?" The answers: Bring a choice of a red and a blue blouse (the idea that if I wear blue, Julia will wear red), and they will supply an apron. It wasn't necessary to bring along any equipment or food supplies. They had their Irving Street basement in Cambridge stocked with every imaginable tool and ingredient, not to mention what looked like a full kitchen complete with extra help.

When I arrived, I thought the house looked like it was on life support because of all the monstrous tubes snaking into the house through windows and doors blowing cool air in. It was a sultry-hot July day in Cambridge,

Massachusetts, and with all the cooking and baking and equipment going full blast, the house and its occupants needed an extra boost in the air-conditioning.

The kitchen was set up as a photo studio, complete with burning-hot lights, reflectors, and cameras on tripods. The center table had become a work space. There was a stool to one side on which Julia perched just close enough to the action so she could poke her fingers into whatever I was mixing for a taste, or reach to feel the consistency of a dough—always offering a positive reaction in her nasal, heady voice. It felt like my mother was sitting there—all eyes and ears.

My face was smoothed with makeup and dusted with powder, my eyes outlined with eyeliner, which I wasn't accustomed to using. A stylist set every strand of my hair in place, added just the right amount of lipstick, and I was deemed camera ready. I was put into place behind the counter, my ingredients and tools to the right and left, the microwave behind me, and a bowl of berries ready for cooking. Yet something was wrong—my white hair reflected too much, creating a lighting problem. So to correct the problem, the top of my head was dusted with a black powder. We were set!

With Julia Child on her cooking show.

We broke for lunch in the little patio space outside the house. At one point Julia remarked after I made a comment about her lovely home, "When we bought this place we spent sixty-nine thousand for it. Now they tell me it's worth a million!" In the same manner she couldn't quite understand that everybody knew who she was.

It was a great day in Cambridge. I left for home in Minnesota on a high! When my youngest brother called me that evening and asked where I had been, I excitedly replied, "I just filmed a cooking show with Julia Child!"

His response, "Who's Julia Child?"

I guess you still can get a fair trial in this country.

Quick Method Danish Pastry

3½ to 4 cups all-purpose flour
1½ cups (3 sticks) chilled unsalted butter
2 packages active dry yeast
½ cup warm water
½ cup heavy cream or undiluted evaporated milk
½ teaspoon freshly crushed cardamom seed (optional)
½ teaspoon salt
2 eggs, room temperature
¼ cup sugar

Measure 3½ cups flour into a bowl or work bowl of food processor with steel blade in place. Cut the butter into ¼-inch slices and add to the flour. Process or cut the butter into the flour until the butter is about the size of kidney beans.

In a large bowl, dissolve the yeast in the warm water. Let stand 5 minutes. Stir in the cream or milk, cardamom, salt, eggs, and sugar.

Turn the flour-butter mixture into the liquid ingredients, and with a rubber spatula mix carefully just until the dry ingredients are moistened. Cover and refrigerate 4 hours, overnight, or up to 4 days.

Turn the dough out onto a lightly floured board; dust with flour. Pound and flatten to make a 16- to 20-inch rectangle. Fold into thirds, making 3 layers. Turn dough around and roll out again. Fold from the short sides into thirds. This should result in a perfect square. Repeat folding and rolling again if you wish.

Wrap and chill the dough 30 minutes or as long as overnight. For filling, shaping, and baking, follow directions in the following recipe.

Danish Pastry Braid

1 recipe Quick Method Danish Pastry

Butter Cream Filling

¼ cup (½ stick) soft butter
1 cup powdered sugar
¼ teaspoon almond extract
1 cup finely pulverized almonds
1 (3-ounce) package almond paste
1 egg white

Glaze

1 slightly beaten egg
2 tablespoons milk or water
Pearl sugar or crushed sugar cubes, for topping
Chopped or sliced almonds for topping

Icing

1 cup powdered sugar
2 to 3 teaspoons warm water
½ teaspoon almond extract

Cover two baking sheets with parchment paper or lightly grease and flour them.

Divide the chilled dough into 2 parts. Roll each part out to make a rectangle 12 by 6 inches. Place these strips on the prepared baking sheets.

To make the filling, cream the butter and sugar until light. Blend in the almond extract, almonds, almond paste, and egg white.

Spread filling down the length of the center of the strips. Cut slanting strips at ¾-inch intervals along both sides up toward the center using a pastry wheel. Fold strips over the filling in a crisscross manner.

Preheat the oven to 400°F.

Let strips rise for 15 to 30 minutes, just until the pastry strips look puffy; they will not double.

To make a glaze, beat the egg with the milk or water. Brush the pastry lightly with it. Sprinkle the sugar and/or sliced almonds over the top.

Bake about 15 minutes or until golden.

Frost, if desired, with almond-water icing. Blend the sugar, water, and almond extract until smooth and thin enough to drizzle over the braids.

Makes 2 filled braids

On TV with Martha Stewart

People often ask me, "What is Martha really like?"

My answer: "I was really impressed. She's very smart, a quick learner, polite, and very businesslike—also she is so organized. I felt like I had to clean house when I got home!" You know the kind—people who have their homes so perfect that your own home looks like a mess!

It wasn't long after my appearance on Julia Child's show that I got a call asking if I would like to tape a cooking show with Martha Stewart. Again, as with Julia Child, I felt so privileged and wondered "Why me?"

So I offered to do a Finnish holiday coffee table and Norwegian lefse. For this I needed to do a lot of baking preparation as well as pack materials for the trip. I baked my pulla (Finnish cardamom bread), a selection of butter cookies, Finnish prune stars, and sponge cake layers, which I planned to put together on camera. In addition, I packed my lefse equipment, potatoes, butter, and cream. I hardly had room in my bags for a toothbrush and nightgown!

I checked in at the Duluth airport on the e-ticket that had been issued to me. Time to board, and I was in row 2, seat B. I didn't think too much about it, as the plane was one of those puddle jumpers that a large percentage of the flights from Duluth are. When I checked in for my Minneapolis to LaGuardia flight, I was in row 3, seat B. Wow! I was being sent first class—nice wide seats and orange juice in a real glass!

An assistant of Martha's met me at LaGuardia. The drive to Martha Stewart's Westport, Connecticut, studio took about an hour. The studio itself looked like a big farmhouse, but inside it had no feeling of a home. It was more of a large space broken into different areas—a big square in the center of desks and computers, surrounded by more offices, each housing key people in the operation.

It was a maze of file cabinets and storage areas. Everything was labeled, stored, and sorted into specific areas. When I commented about the tidiness of her studio, Martha remarked that she would never find anything if it weren't organized.

The same was true of the kitchen: a bank of stainless steel shelving in one corner and at the end of it a deep sink and counters, with multiple restaurant-style gas ranges lining one wall while refrigerators lined another. There were two long worktables with banks of drawers all labeled and well organized with tools of all kinds. Just off the kitchen was Martha's private restroom, complete with a shower, tub, and vanity.

Martha's office was done in pale green—her signature color—and had a unit with narrow drawers and a large table in the center they used for conferences. Everything was all done in high-gloss paint.

When I finally met Martha, it was over a kitchen counter. I presented her with a slab of lutefisk and she was delighted. She said she would turn it over to her Norwegian sister-in-law, who would be preparing their family Christmas dinner.

We unpacked my bags—fortunately everything was in fine shape and I was able to place all of the baked goods on the beautifully set table. Because Martha's sister-in-law is Norwegian, the table was set with classic blue-and-white cups, plates, and saucers.

I proceeded to explain the layout of the Finnish holiday coffee table. There are three basic "courses." For the first course, the guest selects a slice of the cardamom-flavored coffeebread (no spread or butter on it). The next course is a sample slice of an unfrosted cake—like a pound cake or a spiced fruit cake—and you are permitted to choose a cookie or two, to go with your second cup of coffee. With the third cup of coffee (I might mention that the coffee cups hold about 5 ounces), you are permitted to sample the fancy filled cake.

The next thing I did was demonstrate the making of the fancy filled cake. I used Katja's recipe, which was from a girl we had hosted as a Finnish high school student in our home several years before. Katja came home from school one day saying she would like to bake a birthday cake for her friend. She went on to make the cake using basic proportions. Measure the eggs, then add an equal amount of sugar, beat until light and lemon colored, and fold in an equal amount of flour. A pinch of salt, a splash of vanilla—and that's it!

What a revelation! I explained that since then, I have used this "basic proportion" cake to make cakes large enough to serve fifty and small enough to serve just four. In the kitchen at First Lutheran in Duluth we have a commercial-sized mixer, and I used it to make huge batches of sponge cake based on three quarts of eggs and baked the cakes in commercial-sized bun pans to make a celebration cake for a hundred people. The proportion always works!

Martha thought this was a superb idea.

We broke for lunch. A healthy salad and soup, a menu that Martha chose every day and had available for all of her employees.

After that, we went on to my lefse-making demonstration. I was concerned that we cook the correct kind of potatoes (russets) just the proper length of time (until they were soft but not mushy). When the potatoes reached the

With Martha Stewart on her show.

exact doneness, Martha got the hiccups and we had to delay the procedure a good five minutes!

The demonstration went on, then, uninterrupted. We drained, riced, and mashed the potatoes with cream, butter, a bit of sugar, and a bit of salt. I carefully explained that the mashed potatoes should be chilled overnight uncovered.

So, when the potato mixture was chilled and ready, we mixed in the flour and started rolling out the flat potato breads, cooking them on the special griddle I had brought with me. This is a procedure people often have trouble with—but Martha was able, on her second try, to roll out a perfectly round, delicate lefse. I congratulated her on being a quick learner!

Katja's Birthday Sponge Cake

Several years ago we had an exchange student from Finland whose mother is a fabulous cook. One day, Katja asked my permission to bake a birthday cake for her friend and said that she had the recipe. Of course, I thought it was a great idea. I explained the "baking corner" in the kitchen, showed her where I kept my baking tools—measuring cups and spoons, pans, bowls, and the like—then helped her set the oven.

Katja proceeded to take down three identical glass tumblers and pulled out the electric mixer and one springform pan. She cracked eggs into one glass, poured sugar into a second to the same level as the eggs, and added flour to the third one, again at the same level. Hmm. "So much for measuring cups," I thought.

"Oh, dis is the vay vee make birthday cake," she explained. She proceeded to whip the eggs and sugar together until they were very, very light. Then she carefully mixed in the flour. A pinch of salt and a bit of vanilla added, and she poured the batter into the pan and baked it.

It's baking by proportion and I love this recipe! In fact, I don't need to use a recipe at all, but just remember to use an equal measure of eggs, sugar, and flour. Using this simple formula, I've made everything from a single-layer cake to cakes for a hundred. Instead of a springform pan, though, I use regular 8- or 9-inch round layer pans, something that is not commonly used in Europe. Or, if I'm making a half-sheet-pan-sized cake, I use rimmed cookie sheets and multiply the recipe by three times for a double layer 12½- by 17½-inch cake. The baking time and temperature are about the same.

For an irresistible cake, fill it with whipped cream and fresh strawberries or any berries or fruit that is in season. Right now, I'll rely on homemade strawberry or raspberry jam and whipped cream—or I'll splurge and fill the cake with cloudberry jam from Sweden or Finland.

1½ cups (about 6) large eggs, room temperature
1½ cups granulated sugar
Pinch of salt
1 teaspoon vanilla
1½ cups all-purpose flour

Filling and topping

2 cups whipped cream, slightly sweetened
1 cup strawberry, raspberry, apricot, or cloudberry jam or 1 pint fresh berries
4 to 6 tablespoons cloudberry liqueur, Swedish punsch, or light rum
(optional)

Preheat the oven to 350°F. Line the bottoms of two 9-inch round cake pans with parchment or brown paper rounds.

In the large bowl of an electric mixer, beat the eggs until fluffy. Turn speed to high and gradually add the sugar, the pinch of salt, and the vanilla. Continue beating at high speed at least 5 minutes until the mixture is very light and lemon colored. Turn speed down to low and add the flour gradually, mixing just until it is incorporated.

Pour the batter into the two prepared cake pans evenly. Bake for 25 minutes or until the centers bounce back when touched and a toothpick inserted into the center comes out clean and dry. Remove from the oven and cool on a rack.

Loosen edges of cake with a knife and ease the first layer onto a cake plate. Have whipped cream and jam or berries ready. Remove parchment paper from cake. With a long serrated knife, split each layer into two parts. Drizzle with liqueur if desired. Layer with whipped cream and jam or berries. Top with whipped cream. Refrigerate until ready to serve.

Makes about 12 servings

Peachie, the Butter Spokesperson

It wasn't long after my appearances with Julia Child and Martha Stewart that I was selected as the American Dairy Association's "butter spokesperson." Given that I grew up steeped in dairy products on the farm in Floodwood—where our beloved cows were our first and only dairy providers—this was a very easy message for me to relay when I went on a media tour.

I felt like a queen! I was escorted on my travels to different towns and cities across the country by a local food person who made samples of cookies and samples of cookie gift packs to leave behind with each media contact. The cookies and gift packs made great visual props. The American Dairy Association was so organized that all I had to do was show up.

Whenever one is on a media tour there is a chance of being preempted by some major event. It happened to me in Cleveland when last-minute breaking news of a murder flashed across the screens and both of the anchors of the program were away at the crime scene.

Usually, I was scheduled on the early-morning news show. That meant I had to be up at 4:00 A.M. to be picked up at about 5:00 in order to be all bright-eyed and bushy-tailed at 6:00 A.M. The live segment usually ended up being between two and four minutes long.

I would leave behind a basket of cookies with a recipe leaflet, plus another one with butter cookie dough for the producer to take home and bake.

Here's a typical schedule. After the six o'clock morning news in Des Moines, I'd head out for another television station and another live interview and demonstration—again perhaps four to five minutes long. Another basket of cookies and one with dough. At 8:10 A.M. in Des Moines I would have a live phone-in radio interview that would then air in Indiana.

At 9:30 I was off to another ABC affiliate to tape a thirty-minute segment for a program called *Information Iowa*. There I left behind another basket of cookies and a basket with dough, a leaflet, recipes, and a copy of my *Great Holiday Baking Book*.

At 10:15, I was back to my hotel room for a live USA Radio Network interview about baking for the holidays.

At 11:00 A.M., I would have a ten-minute phone-in segment for an ABC affiliate radio station—again, about baking for the holidays.

At 11:15 A.M., I was scheduled to arrive at the NBC TV station to do a live four-minute segment on *Noon News* beginning at 12:15.

After that, at 1:30 P.M., I met with the food editor of the *Des Moines Register* to talk about holiday baking again and the cookie brochure filled with butter cookie recipes that I had developed.

Phew. And onward from there on the tour, I had a similar schedule in Oklahoma City, Nashville, Cincinnati, Cleveland, and Salt Lake City.

One evening in Cincinnati, I appeared on an hour-long informal radio show called *Everybody's Cooking* for which we were squashed into a tiny studio with a couple of rather comic hosts. Half of the show featured a pair of brothers who were sausagemakers. I followed with baking and cooking with butter.

Another time, because of the rather obscure location of the radio station, I was thankful I wasn't driving. The driver took me on a bumpy, narrow road that was built up on sandy flats to a windowless building in the middle of nowhere that looked like a bomb shelter. And the interior was like the dorm room of a college student with sparse furnishings and piles of stuff on the floor.

I had gone on other media tours, too—promoting my own books. I remember once when I took a train to a cable television station somewhere in New England. I boarded the train at Grand Central Station in New York City, having first mixed up bread dough in my hotel room so that it would be rising during my travel. The train was delayed because an earlier one had jumped the track. By the time I got to my destination, I hardly had time to set up my demonstration—I just came running into the studio with my Tupperware bulging with dough and had had to improvise from there.

You never know where milking cows will get you.

Cookie Questions

Over the years, I've answered lots of questions about cookies and cookie baking, and I'd like to share some tips here. Drop cookies are my favorite everyday cookies because the dough is mixed just before baking. All three of my childhood-favorite cookies fall into this category.

Sugar as opposed to excess shortening makes cookies spread out and get brittle. I often cut back on sugar in popular cookie recipes to improve the flavor and texture.

Butter is best for baking flavorful and consistently textured cookies. Margarine is unpredictable because of the different amounts of liquid and different kinds of fat in the product. Shortening itself adds no flavor to cookies, but changes the texture of cookies—you'll notice that cookies made with shortening have a rounded edge rather than a flat edge. Some recipes call for a combination of butter for the flavor and shortening for the texture. Lately, I've opted for one hundred percent butter for health reasons.

Expect cookies made with baking powder to have a softer texture than those made with baking soda as a leavening agent. Baking soda needs to be balanced by some acid ingredient (such as lemon juice, cream of tartar, or even brown sugar) or the cookies will have a brownish color and baking soda taste. Cookie recipes that call for baking soda are usually crispy rather than soft.

As far as cookie sheets go, I like the thin, noninsulated, rimless kind. It doesn't matter if the cookie sheets are dark or shiny, as I am a firm advocate of baking cookies on parchment paper because the cookies brown evenly on the top and the bottom. When I bake cookies on an insulated baking sheet, the tops brown but the bottoms don't.

One last thing: if a cookie recipe calls for milk or another liquid, it is important not to overmix the batter or the cookies will be tough rather than tender.

Chocolate Chip Cookies

2¼ cups all-purpose flour
1 teaspoon baking soda
2 sticks (1 cup) butter, softened
¾ cup packed dark brown sugar
½ cup granulated sugar
2 large eggs
1 teaspoon vanilla
2 cups (12-ounce bag) semisweet chocolate chips
1 cup chopped walnuts or pecans

Preheat the oven to 375°F or convection oven to 350°F. Cover three thin, rimless, uninsulated baking sheets with parchment paper.

Stir flour and baking soda together; set aside. In large bowl, blend the butter with the brown sugar and granulated sugar until creamy. Beat in the eggs and vanilla. Add the flour mixture, chocolate chips, and nuts, and mix until well blended. Drop by spoonfuls onto the prepared baking sheets.

Bake for 10 to 11 minutes in a regular oven, or bake all three pans at the same time in the convection oven for 8 to 9 minutes.

Makes about 5 dozen cookies

The Great River Road

One summer not many years ago Dick and I decided to take a trip along the Mississippi River, down one side and up the other, to explore the region. My interest was mainly the food, and Dick's the geology—and between the two there was lots to enjoy. The Great River Road was established in 1938 and follows the course of the Mississippi River from northern Minnesota to the Gulf of Mexico. It is nearly three thousand miles long and touches on ten states, numerous parks, and historic sites. Driving the Great River Road is one of the most fascinating vacations one can have, but you do have to take the time to enjoy the local events as you meander through the countryside.

There's a seaside atmosphere running right down the center of this great country. River villages, such as Cape Girardeau, Missouri, and Port Gibson, Mississippi, perch spectacularly along the river and there are huge floating hotels like the Mississippi Queen that create a festive scene as they chug into small-town ports. The scenery varies from rolling hills to rocky cliffs, as well as lofty arched trees—perfect places for picnics.

One observation was how the Civil War seemingly came to life as we crossed the state borders going south. In Galena, Illinois, we checked into the restored mansion given to General Ulysses Grant and his family following the Civil War. A tour of the house hinted at the theme we followed during the trip—the living history of the Civil War.

From Galena southward, catfish—the most popular of the "fresh fish"—was prominent on menus. It was usually deep fried with a golden crust. I remember, as a kid, throwing the ugly catfish back into the St. Louis River in favor of northern pike and walleye.

We bumped along in our Honda Civic to the next town of Nauvoo, Illinois, which was founded by the Latter-day Saints in 1839. Its temple stands high on a bluff overlooking a bend in the Mississippi River and is a reproduction of the original nineteenth-century temple that was damaged by fire in the mid-1800s. Curiously, Nauvoo is famous for three things: wheat bread and pastries, blue cheese, and wine. Here we enjoyed a delicious wheat-and-nut coffeecake, and I begged the bakery for the recipe—which they conveniently pointed to in a recipe book on their shelves. I reworked the recipe, as chef's recipes rarely turn out at home exactly as they're made at a restaurant. Here is my version of a classic Nauvoo wheat-and-nut coffeecake.

Farther on down the River Road in New Orleans we happened upon a cooking school just in time to enroll for a demonstration on preparing okra gumbo, shrimp creole, Caesar salad, bananas Foster, and café brûlot. Our instructor was a native Creole and explained Creole as being a blend of French, Spanish, American Indian, and African cookery. From the French came basic knowledge of fine cookery, and because the French settlers had

Nauvoo Wheat-Nut Coffeecake

Topping

½ cup packed brown sugar
½ cup whole wheat flour
1 teaspoon cinnamon
Good handful of walnuts, chopped
3 tablespoons soft butter

Cake

1 egg
½ cup sugar
½ cup milk
3 tablespoons soft butter
1½ cups whole wheat flour
Pinch of salt
2½ teaspoons baking powder

Preheat the oven to 350°F. Butter a 9-inch square cake pan and set aside.

For the topping combine the brown sugar, whole wheat flour, and cinnamon in a bowl; stir in the walnuts and butter, until mixture looks like coarse bread crumbs.

In another bowl, beat together the egg and sugar and mix in the milk and butter. Blend in the flour, salt, and baking powder.

Turn batter into the prepared cake pan and sprinkle evenly with the topping. Bake for 25 minutes or until a toothpick inserted into the center of the cake comes out clean and dry.

to adapt recipes to use local ingredients, many of the techniques involved are somewhat classic French. From the Spanish came a gusto for piquancy and the use of various peppers from mild to hot. Africans contributed "slow cooking" methods, according to our teacher, because the native cooking vessel was a huge clay bowl. From local Indians came the gift of herbs and spices.

As he chopped and mixed and stirred, the instructor explained that long, slow cooking produces mellow and delicious flavors. Quoting his mother, he drawled in his Southern accent, "You dooze it until it beeze right."

I collected the recipe for shrimp creole from him, and back in Minnesota I revised the recipe, and further, I serve it with wild rice. I figured if everyone can make changes in the original, I can too!

Shrimp à la Creole

¼ cup vegetable oil
1 (6-ounce) can tomato paste
1½ cups chopped celery
1½ cups chopped onion
1½ cups chopped green pepper
½ cup chopped green onion
3 cloves garlic, minced
1 (15-ounce) can tomato sauce
3 bay leaves, crumbled
1 teaspoon dried thyme leaves, crushed
1 to 2 pounds raw, peeled shrimp (the more the better, I feel)
Dash cayenne pepper, or more if you like
Salt to taste
Cooked wild rice or fluffy white rice for serving

In a heavy Dutch oven, heat the oil and add the tomato paste. Cook, stirring, for 20 minutes.

Add the celery, onion, green pepper, green onion, and garlic. Add the tomato sauce, bay leaves, and thyme and simmer, stirring occasionally, for 2 hours or until the mixture is thickened.

Add the shrimp, cayenne, and salt. Simmer 15 minutes, until shrimp is pink.

In the meantime, cook the rice. Serve the creole over rice.

Makes 6 servings

The Butter Churn and
My Beloved Mom

I sat at the table with my aging mother, playing our daily game of Scrabble. Scrabble kept her mind alive, but her shoulder cracked as she strained to reach the corner of the board, seizing every opportunity to cover each corner and grab the triple-point spot each time I came within four squares of it. Then she would ask me, "How much are you ahead now?"

"Mom," I'd say, "you're fifty-four points ahead." "Oh, you just let me!" she would exclaim. Although she would never admit it, she always was competitive. For instance, even as her eyesight was failing she wanted to prove she could still read. She would read signs while I drove her to a clinic appointment or to visit her sister at the Chris Jensen nursing home in Duluth. I could usually predict which ones she would read out loud: "Bigger better bagels; a dollar thirty-one for gas, it's gone down three cents; men working; yield . . . drive-through window?"

As we played Scrabble I sipped my herbal tea and she, her hot apple cider. She never cared for tea. "Tastes funny," she would say.

Outside, one of the kids was cutting the field grass, making large swirled cuts with the riding mower. What we call our lawn is really an old field, once a pasture for cows. It's mostly dandelions, hawkweed, plantain, and quack-grass. But the smell of the newly cut greens is sweet, and when the mower makes a swipe by the mint-gone-wild, the aroma floats into the house.

On the table next to the Scrabble board I had placed our old Dazey butter churn, still in perfect condition but long out of use. I took it down from its perch on the shelf because it needed dusting. (I'm a stream-of-consciousness housekeeper—if I notice something needs to be done I do it right away.) As I looked at my mother, and at the butter churn, my mind floated back to my childhood days.

The hunched woman sitting across from me, trying to figure out how to make words with a shortage of vowels, was once seven inches taller and forty pounds heavier and stood tall and strong. She would skim the rich, heavy cream at the top of chilled fresh milk from the prior evening's milking, then pour it into this very churn. It was my job to churn it into butter. If the cream was too warm, it wouldn't turn into butter, which made churning an early-morning job in the summertime.

I think back: I'm ten years old. I sit on the front steps of the farmhouse where I grew up, turning the crank that makes the paddles inside the glass jar spin. The cream splashes up and coats the little removable screen on the top of the churn. My eyes quickly shift left and right. Nobody's watching. I lift the little screened lid and lick it clean, then quickly snap it back into place.

Fresh cream has always been my favorite food. I savor the texture, the sweet aroma, and with my tongue rub its richness all over inside my mouth. There's a faint grassy taste. The cows have been out to pasture, and the cream tastes different when they feed on fresh grass.

The cream finally begins to thicken, then separates into solids and liquid. I drain away the watery liquid and turn the pale yellow butter into a heavy crockery bowl. With a wooden spoon I press the butter together, pressing out more and more of the excess liquid. I sprinkle a little salt over the butter—about a half teaspoonful—and work it into the shiny, smooth mass. At this point a creamery might have added annatto to color the butter a deeper yellow. I dimple the top with the tip of the spoon, cover it, then put it into the icebox.

Mom baked huge batches of rye bread almost every second day, summer and winter. Later, when the loaves came out of the oven of the woodstove, I'd cut a thick slice and slather it with fresh butter. The melting stream of gold ran through my fingers and almost to my elbow, except that I'd lick it off my arm.

My dad even buttered the chocolate cake he cut out of the 9- by 13-inch cake pan with a spoon. That wasn't so bad, but Uncle Frank buttered his doughnuts. We never buttered the pulla, the Finnish cardamom bread. It didn't need it.

Now, these many years later, there is my aging mother, across the table from me, playing a game that she never had the time for in earlier years. I am so privileged to be here.

Twenty-Nine Cookbooks and Counting—All of Them "Pot Boilers"

Each and every book I've written has been the result of a special interest of mine.

My first book, *The Finnish Cookbook,* came together after spending a year in Finland and asking questions about the food, living patterns, celebrations, holidays, and differences in the localities around the country. It was published in 1964 by Crown Publishers after having been recommended to Herbert Michelman, the editor in chief, by Proctor Melquist of my then-employer *Sunset* magazine and a personal friend of Herbert. Proc was the head of *Sunset*'s publishing system and took a liking to my work, much to my thankfulness. He was a tall, rather gangly man with deep wrinkles on his cheeks and forehead and eyes that seemed to pierce one's personality. I always felt a little giddy around him—especially the day when I came in with a huge mushroom of a loaf of Finnish Easter bread, which I had baked in a pail. It caught his attention. This rather entertaining shape for a loaf of bread did not please one of the editors in the food department, as she thought it was a bit corny. The recipe was published and was well received by the magazine's readers.

When we left Menlo Park in the late summer of 1964, I mourned as I would at the funeral of a loved one. But I had to leave, as women did in those days, because my husband, Dick, had just received his PhD at Stanford and had accepted a professorship at the University of Minnesota Duluth. I immediately began to figure out what I could do that was as much fun as working at *Sunset* had been.

The Finnish Cookbook came out about a month later. After much deliberation, I figured I'd try to follow it up with another book. It was much easier to get the attention of a publisher now because my first book had been acclaimed as a success—not because it sold a million or even thousands of books, but primarily because it was original research into an area of the world little known to most. Herbert Michelman at Crown was receptive, so I suggested a cookbook that featured cooking for two.

While I worked at *Sunset,* Dick and I often had special meals for two at home. We did not have the money to entertain ourselves at the number of

I love this photo of Greg, watching me cut a loaf of Easter bread for Sunset *magazine. Photograph by Glenn M. Christiansen; courtesy of Sunset Publishing Corporation.*

wonderful restaurants in the Bay Area and San Francisco, so I would just pretend that the meal was being served to us in a cozy little place.

These meals were always in our student apartment. Cathy and Greg weren't interested in such things as escargot, candlelight, and special cuts of meat and seafood, so I allowed them to select their own menus and eat wherever they wished. Sometimes it was a picnic under the table or under the Meyer Lemon trees outside the apartment. Then I would set the table with the fanciest of dishes—they really weren't *that* fancy, although I did splurge on some very unusual dishes at rummage and estate sales—and we'd enjoy a delicious, special dinner for two with a half-bottle of a nice California wine. After we moved to Duluth, I continued our tradition of Saturday night dinners for two, with special kids' dinners for Cathy and Greg. Thus was born the "gourmet cooking for two" book I proposed to Herbert Michelman. He liked the idea, a contract was signed, and I agreed to finish the book within the year.

In the meantime, we had made new and wonderful friends back in Duluth. It was during the fondue craze of the late 1960s, back when a fondue pot was the ubiquitous wedding gift. We fondued on New Year's Eve, kids and all, friends bringing their Sterno-fired pots in which we cooked beef tenderloin chunks in hot oil and ate them with special sauces that I made. We fondued on cross-country ski trips and whenever we got together for special occasions. So I suggested a "fondue menu and party book," and Michelman again accepted the idea. Another book was on its way, and for it I expanded the technique of fondue to include a number of different menus. I went beyond beef and cheese fondues to cooking everything from chicken, pork, lamb, turkey, seafood, and even tofu in oil. A section on cheese fondue opened the idea for all kinds of dunking sauces: from pizza-flavored to Asian, Mexican, Middle Eastern, and other themes. A third style of fondue emphasized desserts, some of which are still popular today—especially chocolate fondue and fruits. Along with sauces, I included fondue side dishes—salads, breads, appetizers, and desserts—all of which expanded the book into one that had a wide variety of uses. *The Complete Fondue Menu and Party Book* sold all right after its publication in 1972, but it came out just a bit later than the big craze and was not a "barn burner."

Around that time I had our third child, we had opened our restaurant in Duluth called Somebody's House, and my time was taken up with everyday duties. I had been called to be a cohost of a locally produced half-hour television show called *Holiday House*. The pay was dismal—in fact, I spent more on babysitting than the seven dollars I got each day to be on the show. Producers of the show had promised me that financial compensation would come from endorsements of products—a promise that never materialized.

Almost a full decade passed before I returned to book writing. Herbert Michelman had by then retired, and my connection to Crown Publishers was gone.

In the seventies *Sphere* magazine had come into being and was being published in Chicago. The editor of the magazine contacted me, and I traveled to Finland with the *Sphere* crew to help them with a whole issue on Finnish foods, arts, and entertaining. I ended up writing most of the magazine's stories, although I got credit for only one of them.

On that trip we stayed at the Kalastajatorppa, a high-class Helsinki hotel. I was not included in the evening parties, before-dinner drinks, and hors d'oeuvres. Instead, I would take the tram into the center of the city to shop,

eat, and explore. For most of the trip, I interpreted for the staff of the magazine while working and became appalled at the crass attitude of the editor
and writers, who thought they should get everything for free. They refused
to pay for anything, and the Finns were dumbfounded. I found myself apolo-
gizing for their rude behavior. I was stupid enough to accept things as they
were—and all I got out of the trip was the trip itself. In other words, no pay.
The resulting magazine issue from the mid-1970s was gorgeous, even though
the model on the cover was German, not Finnish, and some of the fabrics
resembled Finnish design, but were also German. I didn't say anything.

During my hiatus from book writing, I had become fascinated by the food
processor and the convection oven. At that time I had been making all our
bread at home by mixing the dough in the food processor—baking one loaf
at a time. I recognized that this would be a good topic for a book. At the same
time, I was using the countertop convection oven in a variety of ways. For
these two book project ideas, instead of querying Crown, I reached out to
Publications International in Chicago.

Two books followed. I was paid three thousand dollars for each, plus the
cost of ingredients, and did not have the rights to the books. The first book
was *Food Processor Bread Book*, published in 1980, and the second book came
out the same year under the title *Convection Oven Cookbook*. During my time
writing these books, our kitchen was a scene of amazement for our kids and
their friends as they counted the number of ovens and food processors that
had been lent to me by manufacturers. I didn't get to keep them.

In 1981 I did one of the dumbest things I have ever done: I tried to self-
publish a cookbook. For seven years I had been writing a weekly column in
the *Duluth News Tribune* under the title "The Liberated Cook." The "libera-
tion" came from the idea of using the food processor and microwave oven to
speed up all things leading to dinner. People still tell me that those are some
of their favorite recipes. I was so enthusiastic about the book's prospects that
I had friends lined up to rush more copies to merchants as they ran out of
stock! In the end, I didn't need any "runners," and the book was something
of a bust. I had to borrow money to pay the printing bill—from, of all people,
my parents. Did that ever put a guilt trip on me! It took years to clear off that
bill, and in the meantime I felt I couldn't buy anything or spend money on
anything extra.

It was time, I thought, to get back into writing books again, so I queried
HP Books in Tucson about doing a colorful book on Scandinavian meals.
Scandinavian Cooking appeared in 1983 and was followed in 1985 by *New
Ideas for Casseroles*. Many years later, after those books went out of print, I
requested the rights to them. The University of Minnesota Press has repub-
lished a number of my cookbooks, minus the photographs.

Baking in my kitchen—something I have been doing since I made my first salt cake at five years of age.

I had been baking a lot of whole grain breads during these years, so I queried the idea of a book on the subject. In 1984 Dutton published *Great Whole Grain Breads*, featuring a whimsical "fairy godmother" type of character on the cover with warm colors. It was the beginning of the era of healthy whole grain baking as pioneered by the Tassajara bread book, the Moosewood Restaurant books, and others. I included many of my favorite Finnish-influenced breads, as well as Northern and Eastern European styles of breads.

After focusing on whole grain breads, and interested more broadly in the history of American baking, I proposed a book called *Great Old-Fashioned American Desserts*, which Dutton published in 1987. That book was great fun to research, as I had never read much about the history of ingredients such as Eagle Brand milk or Key limes from Florida. The book came out in a most unappealing dust jacket featuring a woman poking a stick into a pie being baked in a woodstove's oven. I recognized the photo as from a book published on the history of American foods. It had been altered to replace a turkey being baked in the oven with pies.

I was then approached by HP Books to do a book on old-fashioned American cooking. *Country Tastes* appeared in 1988, and in it I managed to use a lot of my favorite recipes from my hometown and recipes gleaned by friends. The University of Minnesota Press republished the book under the title *Great Old-Fashioned American Recipes*. It was the sort of book "down home" types enjoy.

My book *Scandinavian Cooking* was based on typical Scandinavian menus. *Scandinavian Feasts* logically followed and was published by Stewart Tabori and Chang in a large-photo format in 1992. The book was an expensive one for the time. Not long after, the publishers decided to move toward a different type of publishing house, and *Scandinavian Feasts* went out of print. I was offered the opportunity to buy the remaining copies, but the cost would have been equal to our house mortgage at that time, so I bought just a few. The remaining copies were sold to a book remainder company, at which point my royalties stopped. I retrieved the rights to the book, and it was later reprinted, minus the photographs, by the University of Minnesota Press.

In the early 1990s, I began a series of books published by Clarkson Potter, an imprint of Crown Publishing under Penguin Random House. Interestingly, Crown was my very first publisher. Recalling my early years in Floodwood and learning to cook, I began collecting nostalgic ideas and recipes from my youth, when we would always bake something special for year-round holidays. I suggested a book along that theme, and that's how *The Great Holiday Baking Book*, published by Clarkson Potter in 1994, came into being. This was followed by a series of little books, including *Light Muffins, Quick Breads, Light and Easy Baking,* and *Pot Pies. Pot Pies* was a book idea given to me by Clarkson Potter as a peace offering. I had wanted to do a book on favorite cookies, but because Martha Stewart wanted to do a book with the same title, even though she suggested it after I had a contract for it, Martha got to do it. *Pot Pies* was fun to do anyway, and I expanded the idea of pot pies to include many variations and even included innovative recipes.

While writing my next book, *Great Whole Grain Breads by Machine or Hand* (1998), I was talking with my editor at Macmillan about the idea I was hoping to follow up with. I had thought that a book on the topic of "yesterday's bread" would be charming. Besides, I had so much bread after baking each recipe three or four times that I'd have a volume of "day after" bread recipes. However, that editor left Macmillan and gave the idea to another food writer in her new place of employment. That taught me not to say too much about "good ideas" to anybody!

I had been writing articles for a number of years for the magazine of the Cooking Club of America, based in the Twin Cities, when they suggested a whole cookbook based on poultry. *Pure Poultry* was published in 2000 and was a title in their series of cookbooks covering a wide range of topics. It was a "contract book," which meant that I was paid a flat fee—no royalties.

Meanwhile, I had become addicted to cooking, baking, and roasting in a convection oven, having a range that offered the convection option. I discovered that no book had yet been written specifically for standard-sized convection ovens. All I could find were books written for countertop ovens—even one I had written earlier. But there had been at this time a significant breakthrough in cooking technology based on convection cooking. Commercial kitchens had been using it for years, but it hadn't taken off for the home cook. My editor, Jennifer Josephy, with whom I had worked when she was at Little, Brown, was so excited about the book that I got a nice advance on royalties. We did a lovely book, without photographs, explaining and giving directions for cooking in a convection oven. My editors got the idea but marketing didn't. They thought it was an old eighties idea and never pushed the book for the time and energy savings that convection cooking offered. Now, more than ten years later, the book is doing very well.

When I found out that Chronicle Books in San Francisco was interested in a casserole cookbook, the hardest part was trying to think of a good title for it. Brainstorming, I came up with all kinds of crazy names like *Under the Lid* or *Cooking Undercover*. Finally, in desperation, I suggested *555 Casseroles*. Bill LeBlond at Chronicle liked it, but he thought that "555 casseroles were too many"—how about *500 Casseroles*? That name was later changed to *The Best Casserole Cookbook Ever*, because the 500 idea sounded too much like the commercial packagers of cookbooks—who collected recipes, untested, from everywhere and enclosed them between the covers of a book.

But how could I come up with so many new recipes? I couldn't simply develop recipes out of the air—people have to visualize what the final product will be, and some familiarity must be part of it. There needs to be a new twist on the old and familiar. Sometimes that twist is simply a new and quicker way to produce the dish, with an updated feel. Sometimes it means changing the seasoning or making the dish healthier by eliminating sugar, fat, and "artificial" ingredients like canned soup. Sometimes it means switching the protein, vegetable, sauce, or flavor, making it more appealing. My recipes are like children: each is different, each has its own personality, but yet they are identifiable individually—even when they belong to a certain family!

To accomplish 500 casseroles, I first looked up the definition of *casserole* in dictionaries. Here's what I found:

Casserole. 1. A stew or moist food dish cooked slowly at a low heat in a covered pot or dish. 2. A deep heavy cooking pot suitable for use in an oven. 3. A porcelain container used for heating food.

So, I surmised, a casserole is the dish in which the food is cooked or the food cooked in this dish. That could be anything from appetizers to desserts! I ended up with nineteen categories or chapters in the book. I handled each chapter as its own story.

An urge to do my own photography then hit me when I suggested a book I was calling "Mini-Indulgences." This was published in 2009 as *Petite Sweets*. A photographer friend was eager for a project, and we did the photography at my house. It was fun!

Sellers Publishing then had another idea: a little book called *Weeknight Desserts* in 2010. All of these desserts had to be quick, easy, one-bowl, with minimal hands-on time. That meant that cookies in a recipe, if baked, had to all fit on one pan, use mainly pantry ingredients, and include straightforward instructions.

With all those books under my belt, many people have assumed that I must be a millionaire. I enjoy my life—but I'm not a millionaire! How much do I get from a cookbook? Well, let's say a book sells for twenty dollars in a bookstore. The bookstore generally buys that book for ten dollars. My contracts allow from seven to ten percent of the wholesale price. From a twenty-dollar book (assuming the bookstore didn't get a lower price for selling in quantity), my cut ranges from seventy cents to one dollar per book. People often ask me if I would make more if I sold the books myself. Well, yes, that twenty-dollar book would allow me about ten dollars if I sold it myself, although if you buy the same book from a bookstore, it indicates to the bookstore that there is

I own so many cookbooks that I need a ladder to reach them all. Photograph by Tom Wallace. Copyright 2005 Star Tribune.

a demand for the book, and consequently the publisher knows it, too. This is probably why clever people who self-publish make a lot more money on each book—but then you need to pay for the printing and production of the book, buy the books, distribute them, advertise them, and handle the sales. It is a lot of work and as much as I enjoy having a bit of money, I am always embarrassed to sell things!

Having written so many cookbooks also means I'm never too far away from questions about this or that recipe. One day I was en route to a wedding shower for my sister and was running late, as usual, with my arms loaded with the lovely Finnish glass platter that was my wedding gift and a ceramic casserole I offered for the potluck. It was April and winter was still all around us, and my heel found one small piece of ice on the pavement. Down I went.

The casserole didn't spill or break, nor did the platter, but my ankle did. A spiral fracture, as I would soon find out. At the time I wasn't really sure how bad my ankle was, having never suffered such an injury before. I didn't miss the party, though, and won most of the game prizes. After cheesecake and coffee, I decided it was time to go to the emergency room just to check things out, as my ankle was really beginning to throb.

I didn't think my injury was too serious until the doctor said, "We're going to have to screw your bones back together." While I was lying on the stretcher waiting to be wheeled into pre-prep for surgery, the nursing staffer poked her head into the cubicle and asked, "Do you, by chance, have a recipe for deep-dish pizza?"

Break a bone and I still can't get away from cooking questions! This was just the first of many more recipe questions during my stay at the hospital. When I got home with my cast and crutches, we made deep-dish pizza for my homecoming supper.

I do have to get a word in about promoting cookbooks. From time to time I appear on local television to talk about my "latest book." But throughout all those books, no memory ever surpasses the blunder I made when promoting my very first book.

When *The Finnish Cookbook* came out in 1964, it was the most exciting time. My first cookbook! And I got to do some promoting. There was a local television station located in the Bradley Building in downtown Duluth. Marian Key hosted a noontime homemakers' show; she invited me on her program to talk about my new cookbook and demonstrate something from it. She asked me a number of questions about Finnish food traditions. All along I had trouble explaining that Finns have many traditions of their own, even though they do acknowledge good food from other European countries.

Then Marian asked me, "What's the difference between Finnish meatballs and Swedish meatballs?"

My answer? "Finnish balls are bigger."

I didn't realize what I had said, nor did Marian, but the cameramen were practically on the floor laughing. When I got home, Dick said, "Peach, do you know what you said?" Of course I didn't, but I haven't been able to live down my stupid comment!

Cooking in a Church Kitchen
(Bring Sharp Knives!)

Several years ago, when I toured a food company in Chicago, a salesman pulled me aside and asked, "What do you do in Minnesota with all the marshmallows we sell there?" He was a little taken aback by my response: "We put them into green Jell-O and call it a salad. Then we take the salad to a potluck supper at church, where it is served with a macaroni hot dish."

One year, a woman contacted me for suggestions on changing the Lenten Wednesday night suppers at her church. "For way too many years," she said, "we've had a spaghetti bake, lasagna, sloppy joes, chili, and more with lettuce salad bars. It's just too much sameness! Change is difficult for Lutherans, but there must be more to life."

Yes, there can be more to church suppers—or any other large gathering, for that matter. The menu doesn't *have* to have white bread, sliced ham or bologna, sloppy joes or pizza, and iceberg lettuce. It's a perfect venue for a food enthusiast to offer more sophisticated choices.

Times have indeed changed, especially in our church kitchen. It really didn't take that much effort.

What prompted the change was, of all things, the Lenten season, the forty days before Easter. Wednesday night suppers during Lent had become mundane and monotonous. Soup and sandwiches were to be the theme, but nobody wanted to help out or even partake in the meals. We went from canned soups and bologna-and-cheese sandwiches on white store-bought bread to having people make sandwiches at home and then trade them at the supper. Attendance was at an all-time low.

Peter Strommen was our pastor at the time—and he was a master at analyzing situations and empowering people. His plea to me was, "Do something. I don't care what it is, but do something to change the Lenten suppers!"

In rummaging around all the old equipment in the storage room of the church basement, I discovered a twenty-quart Hobart mixer with a whisk and paddle, covered with dust and grime. We brought that up into the kitchen, ordered a dough hook for it, and then we were in the business of mixing bread dough—a project right up my alley!

That was when we started serving homemade bread and offering freshly sliced cheese and cold cuts. This allowed people to make their own sandwiches. Alongside the sandwiches, we served a quickly made soup.

People loved the wild rice bread I had been making at home and bringing to the suppers. It was a recipe I had adapted from one my friend Susan Poupore had created when I worked on a project for the Wild Rice Council. We make that bread in large batches of sixteen loaves at a time. In addition to the wild rice bread we usually make a white bread, fashioned after the recipe we used at Somebody's House, as well as another variety of bread just so people have a choice.

Baking bread fills the entire church with a wonderful, enticing aroma. A couple of years later we began roasting vegetables—mostly root veggies that are in season and available in the late winter/early spring. To round out the menu we made soup. Sometimes a long-simmered split pea, bean, or root vegetable soup—a different variety every week of the six weeks.

Volunteers for the kitchen have found the work rewarding—people come to learn something about different foods, mixing bread dough, all that spiced by the inspiration of being together in a kitchen. Lenten suppers have become an energizing time.

We slice our own cold cuts and cheese instead of buying already sliced and nicely arranged trays. We figure we save a lot of money this way. Men and women with artistic bents can try their hand at creating and arranging beautiful trays of raw veggies, roasted veggies, and sandwich fillings. The results have been amazing.

To round out the meals we have a variety of salads and at least two choices of soups. Nowhere in town can anybody buy such a meal for a "donation." We always hope the donations will cover the expenses. They always have. At least so far.

Besides offering the value of a meal to our guests, there is nothing like working together in a kitchen, scrubbing and peeling carrots, potatoes, and other vegetables, for providing camaraderie. It also has always been fun to introduce new flavors, combinations, and techniques that people can take home and use.

When committees have been formed for the ubiquitous "forward planning" sessions, the cry has routinely been "Don't mess with Lent!" A friend named Marcia, who is a piano teacher, once told me that kids wouldn't schedule their piano lessons on Wednesdays during Lent because of the wonderful community meals at the church.

Church kitchens, however, have one common problem: dull knives! Sometimes we have had all our knives professionally sharpened, but within a couple of weeks, they're all dull again. There are more casualties with dull cutting utensils than with sharp ones. And so the call always goes out: "Bring sharp knives!"

Three-Grain Wild Rice Sunflower Seed Bread

16 loaves	*1 loaf*
1 gallon (16 cups) warm water (about 110°F)	1 cup
2 cups honey	2 tablespoons
⅓ cup active dry yeast	1 package or tablespoon
¼ cup salt	1½ teaspoons
2 cups shortening or oil	2 tablespoons
4 cups uncooked quick rolled oats	¼ cup
4 cups (1 pound) whole wheat flour	¼ cup
4 cups (1 pound) dark rye flour	¼ cup
4 cups cooked and very well drained wild rice*	¼ cup
8 to 10 pounds bread flour	2¼ cups

Glaze and topping

1 egg, beaten with 2 tablespoons water
Toasted, salted sunflower seeds

* Cook 1 cup wild rice according to package directions until very soft; be sure to cool thoroughly before adding to the bread.

Combine warm water, honey, and yeast in large mixing bowl. Let stand 5 minutes until yeast bubbles. Add the salt, shortening or oil, rolled oats, wheat flour, rye flour, and wild rice; mix at low speed until smooth. Slowly add the bread flour; turn mixer on low to medium speed for about 10 minutes or until the dough is well mixed, pulls away from the sides of the bowl, and has a slightly tacky feel. Cover and let rise until doubled (about 1 hour). Divide the large batch of dough into 16 parts and shape each into an oblong or round loaf. Place on lightly greased pans, 4 or 5 per large sheet pan. Cover and let rise until almost doubled, about 45 minutes. Brush loaves with the egg-water mixture and sprinkle with the sunflower seeds. Slash loaves with a sharp blade in two or three places.

Bake in a 375°F regular oven for 35 to 40 minutes, or in a commercial convection oven set at 350°F for about 20 minutes or until a wooden skewer inserted through the loaf comes out clean and dry. Cool on a rack, and slice for serving.

Makes 10 generous slices per loaf

Summing It Up

I have traveled many trends in my lifetime. From the simplicity of the family farm on which I grew up to the scholarly approach of academics to the exploration of heritage and global cuisines, from the confusion of fusion to industry and business to the "chefisms" of nouvelle cuisine and nutritionism, and the influences of television and the media. Cooking for me began on a woodstove on a spartan farm in northern Minnesota, where we prepared meals for hungry hired men who cut lumber with double-handled saws and swamp grass with scythes. At the same time, we cooked for our expanding family. In college, my kitchen journey was further colored by working for a high-class family while being exposed to the world of entertaining dignitaries. It was a difficult transition, then, to cooking as a newlywed and adjusting to meals for two.

Cooking for my own family meant adjusting from preparing meals for two, to three, to four, then five, and entertaining on weekends. All this required a bit of curiosity and flexibility, just as every other stage of my life in cooking did. I suppose, along the way, that publishing twenty-nine cookbooks satisfied my longing to dig a little deeper into many areas of cooking and to explore ideas. Today, the challenge is different. Dick and I are "empty nesters," and although we are cooking for two again, it's different. When we go out to eat, we split a meal or request take-out boxes. We cut a single pork chop into two servings. A big baked potato is enough for both of us. And so the ingredients of my life in and with food keep changing.

When people ask me if I am retired, or when I will retire, my standard answer is, "I don't have anything to retire from!" By definition, retirement is the point when a person stops employment completely. But when you are self-employed, the line is a bit obscured. When does a wife retire from wifehood? Or when does a mother retire from motherhood? And when does a writer and a cook retire?

In truth, it's back to "simple is best" for me in the kitchen, just as it was on the farm in Floodwood growing up. Simple cooking doesn't have to be boring, not with so many ideas, flavors, and techniques to explore today. After

I have been cooking in family kitchens since I was five years old. Home has always been the heart of food to me. Photograph by Bob King/Duluth News Tribune.

all, simple cooking in Minnesota is different from simple cooking in Mexico or India or Sweden or England or any other part of the world. I like to explore the simple cooking of many countries. That is my new passion.

I keep thinking about a greeting card I read years ago. It said, "They tell me I'm a has-been. Was I?"

Beatrice Ojakangas began her writing career as a food editor for *Sunset* magazine and has written for many of the nation's leading magazines, such as *Bon Appétit, Gourmet, Woman's Day, Family Circle, Redbook, Cooking Light, Country Living, Southern Living,* and *Ladies' Home Journal.* She has been a columnist for the *Minneapolis–St. Paul Star Tribune* and the *Duluth News Tribune,* writing about food for the people of Minnesota. She starred in a five-part television series on holiday baking, *The Baker's Dozen,* for the Food Network, and she is the author of twenty-nine cookbooks, including *Scandinavian Cooking, Great Old-Fashioned American Recipes, Great Whole Grain Breads, Scandinavian Feasts,* and the award-winning *Great Scandinavian Baking Book,* all published by the University of Minnesota Press. Her first book, *The Finnish Cookbook,* has been in print since 1964. In 2005, she was selected for the James Beard Cookbook Hall of Fame. She lives in Duluth, Minnesota.